The pattern
of our days

Liturgies and resources
for worship

edited by
Kathy Galloway

First published 1996

Wild Goose Publications
Unit 15, Six Harmony Row, Glasgow G51 3BA

Wild Goose Publications is the publishing division of the
Iona Community.
Scottish Charity No. SC003794. Limited Company Reg. No. SCO96243.

ISBN 0 947988 76 9

Cover illustration 'The pattern of faith' and textual illustrations by
Adrienne Kern, 1996.

Distributed in Australia and New Zealand by Willow Connection
Pty Ltd, Unit 7A, 3-9 Kenneth Road, Manly Vale NSW 2093.
Permission to reproduce any part of this work in Australia or New
Zealand should be sought from Willow Connection.

A catalogue record for this book is available from the British
Library.

Printed by The Cromwell Press Ltd, Melksham, Wilts.

The Iona Community

The Iona Community is an ecumenical Christian community, founded in 1938 by the late George MacLeod (Very Rev Lord MacLeod of Fuinary). Gathered around the rebuilding of the ancient monastic buildings of Iona Abbey, but with its original inspiration in the poorest areas of Glasgow during the Depression, the Community has sought ever since the 'rebuilding of the common life', bringing together work and worship, prayer and politics, the sacred and the secular in an incarnational faith.

The Community today is a movement of around 200 Members, 1,200 associate members and 2,000 Friends. The Members — women and men from many backgrounds, countries and denominations — are committed to a rule of daily prayer and Bible reading, sharing and accounting for their use of time and money, regular meeting and action for justice and peace.

The Iona Community maintains three centres on Iona and Mull: Iona Abbey and the MacLeod Centre on Iona, and Camas Adventure Camp on the Ross of Mull. Its base is in Community House, Glasgow, where it also supports work with young people, the Wild Goose Worship and Resource Groups and a publishing house, Wild Goose Publications. It publishes a bimonthly magazine, *Coracle*.

The worship of the Iona Community

Worship has been fundamental to the life of the Iona Community since it began. It was with the intention of breaking down the barriers between our everyday lives and language and the life of the worshipping community that the first members, ministers and craftsmen engaged together in the rebuilding of the Abbey ruins, began and ended each day with common worship. Work and recreation were encompassed within the pattern of worship, because they are not to be held apart. Each informs the other.

Still on Iona, the pattern remains the same. The continuing group on whose life the daily worship is based is the resident community living in the Abbey and the MacLeod Centre. Their work and that of the guests in the centres, is rooted in worship. We are accountable in all things to God. We make account as a Community in our worship. In the mornings, the worship is the daily service of the Iona Community, during which the members are prayed for by name. Evening worship reflects the concerns of the Iona Community, which are, of course, concerns of the whole Christian community: justice and peace, healing, creation, commitment, community and celebration.

At Camas too, the day is encompassed by worship, either held in the Chapel of the Nets, or outside on the rocks by the water. Camas worship, in the remote and intimate setting of interdependency and dependency on nature, offers unique opportunities for creative worship.

But the worship of the Iona Community does not only take place on Iona. There are many occasions when the Community gathers on the mainland — in the Family Groups which are its base communities; in plenary session in different places; for special events and acts of witness. And each individual Member is committed to working out the rule of the Community in her or his own context of place, work, people, and in their own worshipping community. Therefore, there are many occasions and situations in which the Community is engaged in finding 'new ways to touch the hearts of all' in worship on the mainland.

Because the membership of the Community (and its Associate Members, Friends and staff) come from such a diversity of background, place, faith tradition and experience, the kinds of worship they are involved in is enormously varied. The life and service of the local church, the work of community and campaigning groups, ecumenical and international events, small groups and house churches, are all part of the engagement of Members. All of these are proper places for prayer.

But whether on Iona or at Camas or on the mainland, whether it is the Community gathered or the Community dispersed, there are some features of our worship which are constant.

It is *incarnational.* At its heart is the belief that God in Jesus Christ became a human being like us, sharing fully in all the hopes and fears, joys and sorrows of our lives, to let us know that God loves us, forgives us, makes us whole, desires to give us life in all its fullness. Therefore we believe that there is no part of life that is beyond the reach of our faith. The word of life is as much for our politics as for our prayers.

It is *historical.* It draws on the experience and creativity of our mothers and fathers in the faith. The Celtic church of Columba had a strong and deep sense of the incarnation, and of the glory of God in creation. We share these beliefs in both the Incarnation and the integrity of creation, and they find expression in our worship. We value the Benedictine traditions of hospitality and the centrality of prayer (though we may go about these in very different ways). We drink deeply from the well of Biblical faith of our Reformed forbears. Sometimes we use orders and liturgies which have come down through the ages. They are part of the great drama of worship. They also remind us that we are part of a worldwide church.

It is *ecumenical,* because we are an ecumenical community, and part of a worldwide church. We are constantly receiving gifts from the various traditions represented in our membership, from Quaker and Anglican, Methodist and Baptist, Presbyterian and Roman Catholic. We cannot but be ecumenical. We do not believe this condemns us to the blandness of the lowest common denominator. We believe this challenges us to be open, honest and creative. This, of course, is a constant struggle, and sometimes a source of conflict and pain. But these are the places we grow.

To be ecumenical in its true sense demands that we be *inclusive*. We believe that God welcomes everyone who seeks to worship in spirit and in truth. So it is a matter of faithfulness to God's purposes that people do not feel unwelcome by the use of language which excludes on account of gender, race or culture. Nor should it be the case that our worship can only be understood by people who have degrees in theology, or have grown up in the church. It also means that planning and leadership of worship is not confined to the clergy. Since liturgy is the work of the people, we should not accept this merely as a pious phrase but should make it live, so that the people are fully and actively engaged in worship in songs, responses and open prayer, in symbolic acts, and in the many ways in which it is possible to 'break the Word' in order that it may be shared.

And it is *creaturely*. We are whole people, God's creation, and we want to respond through our senses as well as our intellects. In movement and stillness, through touch and sight and sound, through smell and taste, we are gifted with many ways to pray.

Prayer changes people. Faith changes people. This we believe. Therefore, we try to be *open to change*, to the new, in our worship. God meets us out there on the borders as much as in what is familiar and reassuring.

The Iona Community has been blessed in recent years by the existence and contribution of the Wild Goose Worship and Resource Groups. The songs, liturgical pieces, drama and meditations have found recognition, acceptance and widespread gratitude. Because we as a Community have profited so greatly from the work of the Groups, and had so much access to their creativity, it is sometimes easy to take it for granted. This we do not want to do. It has given us 'a new song to sing'. It has introduced us to the wealth of ways in which the church throughout the world sings its faith, especially the church in the poorest countries of the world. Most of the liturgies in this book incorporate Wild Goose Songs: an index of which, and the music books in which they may be found, is given at the back of this book.

The material in this book, reflects the faith and engagement of a Community which has nurtured both for its Members. We offer it in the hope that it may yield good fruits to those who use it.

This book has been a common task. The editorial group has approached it as a labour of love. My thanks to them: Joanna Anderson, Ruth Burgess, Malcolm King, Cilla McKenna, Kate McIlhagga.

Kathy Galloway
Community House, Glasgow

Foreword

Worship has always been at the heart of the life of the Iona Community. It is the mainspring of all our activities and both the beginning and end of our commitment to world peace, social justice and the rediscovery of a integrated spirituality. We are proud of the publications we have already been producing as resources for the worship of the wider church — the prayers of George MacLeod, succeeding editions of Abbey Worship Books, and the wide range of material produced through the creativity of John Bell, Graham Maule and their colleagues on the Wild Goose Resource and Worship Groups.

For some years there has been a feeling within the Community that we should find an opportunity to complement these by bringing together some of the material produced by Members of the Community. Community Members work and worship in a wide variety of local situations and are involved, whether ordained or lay, in many different worship settings. This book reflects the strength and breadth of the Community's commitment to forms of worship that are inclusive, accessible and rooted in a context of engagement with the life needs and problems of the world. I believe that it will be welcomed and well used among all those throughout Britain and beyond whose support and interest the Community values so much and which I have particularly appreciated since becoming Leader. With our present Membership and the degree of involvement I know exists in developing creative approaches to worship that are appropriate to particular local circumstances, I believe that we as a Community have the capacity to produce several companion volumes to this one and I look forward to their publication in the years ahead!

These are challenging times for the church and exciting times for the Community. Changes continue on mainland and island. The millennium approaches and before that important political and social events will involve both the Community and individual Members. Kathy Galloway and those who have worked with her are to be congratulated on producing this book. I hope that everyone who uses the liturgies and resources in it will find their faith enhanced and their worship enriched.

Norman Shanks
Leader of the Iona Community

Using the book

The first section of the book consists of a number of complete **liturgies**. These are organised under four headings, each one of which represents an important subject or concern in the life of the Iona Community. There is a short introduction to these at the beginning of each heading.

The liturgies can be used complete as they stand, with appropriate amendment and additions to take note of the local context. Or the shape of the liturgy can be used, but substituting other prayers, readings, songs, etc. Or they can simply be used as a source of ideas for other acts of worship.

The second section is headed **resources**. It includes prayers, litanies and responses and a number of readings and meditations. These are arranged, broadly speaking, in a way which reflects the movement of the drama of worship, the great story of salvation, a movement which begins with;

- preparation and approach to God, and the recognition and naming of the brokenness of life;
- God's response in the Word, in scripture, in the witness of those who have met the Word in their lives;
- our response to God's liberating Word made flesh, in prayer for others, in self-offering, in thanksgiving.

In worship, we always begin where we are. In hearing and receiving the Word of life, whether it is one of forgiveness and acceptance, of comfort or challenge, of promise or demand, we are changed. We move to a different place, a place where Jesus is always calling, 'follow me.' In this different place we discover, or remember, that we are part of a Body, in which 'if one part suffers, all the other parts suffer with it, if one part rejoices, all the other parts rejoice with it.' We are most fully ourselves when we are most fully part of the Body.

Therefore our worship sustains most, refreshes most, has the greatest integrity, not when our words are most beautiful, our liturgies most reverent or innovative, our music most heavenly, but when our lives are most fully engaged. It is important that we do not censor 'all that we have and all that we are' in worship, whether that be feelings, imagination, desire, concern, or the limitations and inadequacy that we sometimes experience. It is better that we make of these an offering. We do not have to be perfect, we do not have to be nice, we need to know our need of God.

That is not in any way to say that our worship can be slapdash or ill-prepared. We take care of what we value. If we value the offering of worship, then we want to attend to it with all the care and creativity at our disposal — which is usually much more than we, and sometimes the church, believe.

If this book encourages those who use it to find something more of their own creativity and ability in worship, it will have served its purpose.

Liturgies

Resources

LITURGIES

Pilgrimage and journeys

Each Wednesday on Iona, the Iona Community invites all those staying on the island, whether in the Abbey, the MacLeod Centre or elsewhere, to join in a pilgrimage round Iona, visiting places of historical or religious significance, and reflecting on our own journeys of faith. On the way, we share food, conversation and silence across barriers of age and experience, language and culture. At each stop, there is a short act of worship.

But pilgrimage is not only something on, or to Iona (or indeed to other places of significance for people of faith). Christian faith is often referred to as *the Way* and Christians as *people of the Way*. And indeed, journeys and pilgrimage are powerful human symbols which transcend divisions of religion, culture, history and geography. Home or origin, departure and destination, travel and homecoming, speak a universal human language.

We can conceive of our lives as a journey or pilgrimage, and stages on that journey are marked by ceremony, by rites of passage. And pilgrimage does not need to cover a territory marked out in kilometres. The journey to school or work on the first day may be very long indeed and some of our most demanding journeys take place in the inner landscape of our lives.

The liturgies in this section relate either to the marking in some way of birth and death (particularly aspects of these that sometimes go unregarded in the worship books of our churches) or to pilgrimages that are not measurable in miles. One of these helps us to look at our local church in a different way. The other remembers the Exodus, the going out, of the people of Israel, and of Jesus Christ.

| 1 |

The blessing of children (without baptism)

Opening responses

Leader: In the beginning, God made the world,
light and dark, shape and void, height and depth,
to tell of love

ALL: AND GOD SAYS IT IS GOOD

Leader: In land and sea, in plant and seed,
in growth and decay,
God's love is shown

ALL: AND GOD SAYS IT IS GOOD

Leader: In creatures great and creatures small
in movement and stillness, in birth and death,
God's love is shown

ALL: AND GOD SAYS IT IS GOOD

Leader: In woman and man,
in joy and sorrow, in laughter and tears,
God's love is shown

ALL: AND GOD SAYS IT IS GOOD

Leader: In the gift of new life, in signs of hope,
in the children we are given

ALL: GOD'S LOVE IS SHOWN

Leader: So let us celebrate and give thanks
for the gift of this child/these children

ALL: WITH GOD WE SAY, 'IT IS GOOD'

Leader: Jesus said: Let the children come to me,
do not try to stop them,
for the kingdom of heaven belongs to such as these.

Song

Prayer

Leader: God our Maker,
we praise you for your creation, and especially for
life new and renewed. We rejoice and thank you for
the life of *(name)* given in love to *(name)* and *(name)*
as their child. We pray that *(name)* and *(name)* will, in
their loving, guiding and nurturing of their child be
strengthened and aided by the power and presence of
your love in Jesus Christ.
Amen.

Leader: *(Name)* and *(name)*, will you, with God's help, strive
to share your love, faith, wisdom and understanding
with *(name)* and make for her/him a home where she/
he may learn to live in love, peace and justice?

Carers/
Family: We will.

To all others present

Leader: Will you who form the community of love in which
(name) will grow, keep this child and her/his parents/
carers in your hearts and prayers, and give an example
of faith, hope and love to them all, with God's help.

ALL: WE WILL

*The parents/carers are invited to bless the child first
with these words*

Carers/
Family: May God's joy be in your heart
and God's love surround your living.
Each day and night
and wherever you roam.
May you know God's presence.
In growing and learning,
in joy and sorrow,

in friendship,
in solitude,
in beginnings and endings
may God keep you and bless you
all the days of your life.

They kiss the child/ren

A candle is handed to the child/ren

ALL: THE BRIGHT LIGHT OF GOD'S GUARDING
BE WITH YOU
THE BRIGHT LIGHT OF CHRIST'S LOVE
BE WITH YOU
THE BRIGHT LIGHT OF THE SPIRIT'S PRESENCE
SURROUND AND ENFOLD YOU
ALL THE DAYS AND NIGHTS OF YOUR LIFE.
AMEN.

Song

Closing responses

Leader: Making us, shaping us
ALL: BLESSING US, TRUSTING US

Leader: Leading us, disturbing us
ALL: EMPOWERING US, LOVING US

Leader: God of our childhood
ALL: GOD OF OUR GROWING

Leader: Stay with us on our journey
ALL: AND BRING US SAFELY HOME

2 | *Liturgy for a stillborn child*

As one whom a mother comforts
I will comfort you, says the Lord

We come here to thank God for *(name of child)*
To thank God for his/her conception
To thank God for the months she/he
was carried in *(name of mother's)* womb
and in *(name of father's)* heart;
To thank God that in his/her short life
she/he brought joy and laughter,
anticipation, and hope for the future.

We gather to share our grief
and our anger that a life promised
has been taken; that hope seems
to have been cut off and joy destroyed.

We are here *(as parent[s], grandparents,*
friends and family)
to lay our questions,
our sadness and our hope,
at the feet of Christ,
who opened his arms to receive
all who were wounded and distressed.

We have come to acknowledge
our feelings of guilt and failure,
and to affirm our conviction
that death is not the end,
but a new beginning.

Jesus says: Those who come to me,
I will not cast out.

*Those present are encouraged to give words to their
hopes and fears, their anger, their sadness; to place
flowers, poems, gifts, symbols of love and light on the
coffin or on a nearby table.*

A time of silence and letting go

Chants
Be still and know ■ Lord Jesus Christ, Lover of all

Prayer

Said by all

O God, as *(name of child)*
was cradled in the womb,
cradle her/him and hold her/him
that as we let her/him go,
we may know that he/she has gone
from our loving presence
into yours forever.
In Jesus' name we pray.
AMEN

3 *Liturgy for the anniversary of a death*

*The setting for this liturgy is some kind of shared
gathering, e.g. a family meal, a picnic, a meeting of
friends. The physical setting should be relaxed. The
liturgy is participative, and leadership should be
shared. Take responsibility for each others' feelings.
Laughter and tears are appropriate in this setting.*

Opening responses

Come among us God
You, who cast the planets into space
and cradle the sparrow in her nest
COME GOD AND MEET US HERE

Come among us God
You, who bless the poor and the broken
and stand by the sad and the strong
COME GOD AND MEET US HERE

Come among us God
You, who dance in the silence
and shine in the darkness
COME GOD AND MEET US HERE

Reading

Psalm 139, vs 7 - 10
Where shall I go to escape your spirit
Where shall I flee from your presence?
If I scale the heavens you are there
If I lie flat in Sheol you are there
If I speed away on the wings of the dawn
If I dwell beyond the ocean
Even there your hand will be guiding me
Your right hand holding me fast.

Revelation 21, vs 3 - 4
I heard a voice say: Look,
God lives among human beings
and makes a home among them, they are God's people
and God is their God — God with them.
God will wipe away all tears from their eyes,
there will be no more death and no more
mourning or sadness or pain. The world
of the past has gone.

John 14, vs 1 - 3
Jesus said: Do not let your hearts be troubled.
You trust in God, trust also in me.
In God's house there are many places to live —
if it were otherwise I would have told you.
I am going now to prepare a place for you,
and after I have gone and prepared you a place,
I shall return to take you to myself,
so that you may be with me, where I am.

A space to remember

*A chance to remember those who have died — to retell
stories, to sing songs, to share common memories, to
bring into the present the things we want to recall, to
share silence.*

*Use a ritual action that is meaningful to those present,
e.g. light a candle, place a stone or flower, float petals in
water. Place something centrally that recalls those who
have died.*

All our laughter, all our sadness
SAFE NOW IN GOD'S HANDS

All our anger, all our gladness
SAFE NOW IN GOD'S HANDS

All our stories, all our memories
SAFE NOW IN GOD'S HANDS

Those we remember, those we love
SAFE NOW IN GOD'S HANDS

Sing a song together, listen to some favourite music, have a coffee.

Closing responses

We ask for the love of God
AND THE MESSAGES OF ANGELS

The laughter of Jesus
AND THE STORIES OF THE SAINTS

The power of the Spirit
AND THE STRONG HANDS OF FRIENDS

To bless us on life's journey
AND LEAD US SAFELY HOME.
AMEN [1]

1   *A Book of A Thousand Prayers*, edited by A Ashwin, HarperCollins Publishers

Hope and renewal in times of change: four exodus liturgies

These liturgies are entitled **Home; Exile; Desert; Promised Land.** *They may take place on four consecutive occasions or as one whole act of worship. Thematically, they are appropriate for a number of contexts, since the Exodus journey is a discernable movement in many aspects of human experience, e.g. the passage from childhood through adolescence to maturity, or the stages of community formation.*

It is desirable that people face one another, and that there is a central point where images of each stage are easily visible.

When the four liturgies are taking place as one act of worship, it may be a processing liturgy, somewhat like a Stations of the Cross, whereby the people move from one stage to another, with four points arranged with appropriate images and symbols. During the movement from one stage to another, the following chant may be sung softly :

SEND OUT YOUR LIGHT, LORD,
SEND YOUR TRUTH TO BE MY GUIDE
THEN LET THEM LEAD ME
TO THE PLACE WHERE YOU RESIDE

| 4 | **Home** |

Call to worship

Leader: The Lord says: When the time comes,
           I will answer the prayers of my people

Left: I will betroth you to myself for ever
Right: With integrity and justice, with tenderness and love

Left: I will betroth you to myself with faithfulness
Right: And you will come to know me.

Left: I will say: You are my people
Right: And you will answer: You are our God

Left: For once you were outside mercy
Right: But now you have been given mercy

ALL: THIS IS OUR HOPE, OUR LIVING HOPE
           WE SHALL BE GLAD

Leader: The Lord says: When the time comes,
           I will take back my gifts of corn and wine.

Reading
Genesis 18, vs 1 - 8

Psalm or song
O God, you are my God alone ■ My Shepherd is the Lord ■
The Love of God comes close ■ A Touching Place ■ Come,
Host of Heaven's ■ Take This Moment
■ May God draw near ■ Jesus Christ our living Lord

Symbols of home

Suggestions for these might include a bunch of keys, theatre masks, toys or ornaments, laid out in a central position so that all are able to see and reflect on them.

Silence to reflect

On the varied meanings that 'home' has for each one of us.

A time of witness or exchange about meanings of 'home'.

Chant

Sung softly and repeatedly
MAY THE WORDS OF OUR MOUTHS AND THE
THOUGHTS OF OUR HEARTS
BE ACCEPTABLE TO YOU,
GOD OUR STRENGTH AND OUR REDEEMER.
AMEN. AMEN

Blessing and repentance

Leader: Strong, sheltering God,
we bless you for all the beautiful things of home;
warmth and shelter when the wind outside is bitter
food for the body and for the soul
treasured gifts and treasured memories
stability, acceptance, care.
We bless you for the chance to be ourselves
for the tasks that weave the pattern of our days
for the sweet, familiar round of ordinary things.

ALL: BLESSED ARE YOU, STRONG, SHELTERING GOD

Leader: But if we have forced unfair expectations on others
taken their care for granted
helped to make of a safe place a battleground
or used our belonging to shut others out

ALL: HAVE MERCY ON US,
GOD OF FRIEND AND STRANGER
DISTURB OUR COMPLACENCY
SHAKE OUR CIRCLES OF CONTENTMENT
SWEEP THROUGH OUR HEARTS
AND OUR HOUSES
WITH THE NEW BROOM OF YOUR SPIRIT
UNTIL LOVE IS OUR ONLY REFUGE.
AMEN

Reading

Luke 2, vs 39 -52

Prayers of concern

- for all whose homes are places of unhappiness, threat or insecurity

Chant

LISTEN LORD, LISTEN LORD, NOT TO OUR WORDS BUT TO OUR PRAYER. YOU ALONE, YOU ALONE, UNDERSTAND AND CARE.

- for all whose homes have been broken by family breakdown or by dispossession
- for all who have no home

Closing responses

Leader: On our hearts and our houses
ALL: THE BLESSING OF GOD
Leader: In our coming and going
ALL: THE PEACE OF GOD
Leader: In our life and believing
ALL: THE LOVE OF GOD
Leader: At our end and new beginning
ALL: THE ARMS OF GOD TO WELCOME US
AND BRING US HOME
AMEN [1]

5 | Exile

Call to worship

Leader: The Lord says: When the time comes,
I will answer the prayers of my people

Left: I will betroth you to myself for ever
Right: With integrity and justice, with tenderness and love

Left: I will betroth you to myself with faithfulness
Right: And you will come to know me.

Left: I will say: You are my people
Right: And you will answer: You are our God

Left: For once you were outside mercy
Right: But now you have been given mercy

ALL: THIS IS OUR HOPE, OUR LIVING HOPE
WE SHALL BE GLAD

Leader: The Lord says: I will fence you in with thorns
and build a wall to block the way

Readings
Genesis 47, vs 1-6 ■ Exodus 1, vs 1-14

Psalm or song
*Just as a lost and thirsty deer ■ Contemporary Reproaches ■
Listen Lord ■ Stumbling Blocks and Stepping Stones ■ Beside
the streams of Babylon ■ The Refugees*

Symbols of exile

For many people, exclusion of various kinds — from work, from political freedoms, from good health, or on the basis of race, gender or sexuality — may also be experienced as a kind of exile. Suggestions for symbols might include passports, No Entry signs, photographs. People might have been asked in advance to bring a photograph that is dear to them. At the conclusion of the reflection, these might be attached to a board or banner, to be held in prayer.

Silence to reflect

On the varied meanings that 'exile' has for each of us.

A Time of Witness or Exchange about meanings of 'exile'.

Chant
MAY THE WORDS OF OUR MOUTHS ...

Blessing and repentance

Leader: God beyond borders
we bless you for strange places and different dreams
for the demands and diversity of a wider world
for the distance that lets us look back and re-evaluate
for new ground where broken stems can take root,
grow and blossom.
We bless you for the friendship of strangers
the richness of other cultures
and the painful gift of freedom

ALL: BLESSED ARE YOU, GOD BEYOND BORDERS

Leader: But if we have overlooked the exiles in our midst
heightened their exclusion by our indifference
given our permission for a climate of fear
and tolerated a culture of violence

ALL: HAVE MERCY ON US,
        GOD WHO TAKES SIDE WITH JUSTICE
        CONFRONT OUR PREJUDICE
        STRETCH OUR NARROWNESS
        SIFT OUT OUR LAWS AND OUR LIVES
        WITH THE PENETRATING INSIGHT
        OF YOUR SPIRIT
        UNTIL GENEROSITY IS OUR ONLY MEASURE
        AMEN

Reading

Luke 4, vs 16-30

Prayers of concern

   •   for refugees and political exiles

Chant

LORD JESUS CHRIST, LOVER OF ALL
TRAIL WIDE THE HEM OF YOUR GARMENT
BRING HEALING, BRING PEACE
   •   for all trapped by their own fear and hostility
   •   for all who experience exclusion because of
          poverty, gender, race, religion

Closing responses

Leader: For all that God can do within us
         For all that God can do without us
ALL: THANKS BE TO GOD

Leader: For all in whom Christ lived before us
         For all in whom Christ lives beside us
ALL: THANKS BE TO GOD

Leader: For all the Spirit wants to bring us
         For where the Spirit wants to send us
ALL: THANKS BE TO GOD

Leader: Listen
           Christ has promised to be with us in the world
           as in our worship
ALL: AMEN, WE GO TO MEET HIM [2]

6 Desert

Call to worship

Leader: The Lord says: When the time comes,
I will answer the prayers of my people

Left: I will betroth you to myself for ever
Right: With integrity and justice, with tenderness and love

Left: I will betroth you to myself with faithfulness
Right: And you will come to know me.

Left: I will say: You are my people
Right: And you will answer: You are our God

Left: For once you were outside mercy
Right: But now you have been given mercy

ALL: THIS IS OUR HOPE, OUR LIVING HOPE
WE SHALL BE GLAD

Leader: The Lord says: I will woo you,
and lead you into the wilderness
and speak to your heart

Readings

Exodus 16, vs 1-6, 35-36 and 17, vs 1-6

Psalm or song

Lifting my eyes up to the hills ■ *Veni Sancte Spiritus*
If you believe and I believe ■ *The Temptations*
Come with me, come wander ■ *The Song is love*
How long, O Lord ■ *Travelling the road to freedom*

Symbols of the desert

Suggestions for these might be stones, sand, weeds, broken or rusted things. If there is time, people might be invited in small groups to create desert 'gardens' in bowls of sand, using stones and small pieces of debris. Or, people could be invited to walk silently in a circle, perhaps pausing at 'stations', each with a question written on a large sheet, e.g. 'How long?', 'Where is hope?', 'What shall we pray?' Here they can pray, light a candle or write a response.

Silence to reflect

On the varied meanings that 'desert' has for each one of us.

A Time of Witness or Exchange about meanings of 'desert'.

Chant
MAY THE WORDS OF OUR MOUTHS...

Blessing and repentance

Leader: God of strangeness and desire
we bless you for enticing us
to the last place we wanted to be
the place where we can hide no longer
where we must face our own emptiness
and see our false gods fall.
We bless you for the immeasurable relief
of self-exposure
for the miracle of survival
and for coming to us in unexpected guises

ALL: BLESSED ARE YOU,
GOD OF STRANGENESS AND DESIRE

Leader: But if we have turned in upon our emptiness
refused the risks you require of us
idolised our self-sufficiency
and clung to our captivity

ALL: HAVE MERCY ON US,
GOD WHO WRESTLES AND EMBRACES US
SHATTER OUR ILLUSIONS
REFUSE YOUR COMFORT OF ANGELS
FEED OUR HOPE AND OUR HUNGER
WITH THE ADVENTUROUS FAITH
OF YOUR SPIRIT
UNTIL GRACE IS OUR ONLY SUFFICIENCY
AMEN

Reading

Luke 4, vs 1-13

Prayers of concern

- for those who experience life as a wasteland

Chant

I WAITED, I WAITED ON THE LORD
I WAITED, I WAITED ON THE LORD
HE BENT DOWN LOW AND REMEMBERED ME
WHEN HE HEARD MY PRAYER

- for those who are lost, or without meaning or value in their lives
- for stateless, dispossessed or migrant peoples

Closing responses

Leader: The desert will sing and rejoice
ALL: AND THE WILDERNESS BLOSSOM WITH FLOWERS

Leader: All will see the Lord's splendour
ALL: SEE THE LORD'S GREATNESS AND POWER

Leader: Tell everyone who is anxious
ALL: BE STRONG, AND DON'T BE AFRAID

Leader: The blind will be able to see
ALL: THE DEAF WILL BE ABLE TO HEAR

Leader: The lame will leap and dance
ALL: THOSE WHO CAN'T SPEAK WILL SHOUT

Leader: This is the promise of God
ALL: GOD'S PROMISE WILL BE FULFILLED

| 7 | **Promised land**

Call to worship

Leader: The Lord says: When the time comes,
          I will answer the prayers of my people

Left: I will betroth you to myself for ever
Right: With integrity and justice, with tenderness and love

Left: I will betroth you to myself with faithfulness
Right: And you will come to know me.

Left: I will say: You are my people
Right: And you will answer: You are our God

Left: For once you were outside mercy
Right: But now you have been given mercy

ALL: THIS IS OUR HOPE, OUR LIVING HOPE
          WE SHALL BE GLAD

Leader: The Lord says: When the time comes,
          heaven and earth will answer each other
          and I will love the unloved

Readings

Joshua 4, vs 1 -7, 19-25 ■ Josh. 5, vs 10-12 ■ Isaiah 58, vs 6-12

Psalm or song

Sing to God with joy and gladness ■ Sent by the Lord
Blessed be God ■ O Bless the Lord ■ Heaven and earth
Heaven is singing for joy ■ The God of heaven ■ No-one
will ever be the same

Symbols of the promised land

Suggestions for these might include milk and honey in the comb, bread and flowers, fruits, all of which people may share with one another; or rooting plants, seeds which people might plant; musical [percussive] instruments to make a joyful noise with; paints or clay with which to play.

Silence to reflect

On the varied meanings that 'promised land' has for each one of us.

A Time of Witness or Exchange about meanings of 'promised land'

Chant
MAY THE WORDS OF OUR MOUTHS ...

Blessing and repentance

Leader: God, our passionate life
we bless you for the infinite beauty of created things
sand, wind, wave and the wings of the eagle
for the love of land and people
for the vine and the fruit and the good wine
We bless you for the endurance of hope
for the promise of renewal
and for fleeting moments on the mountaintop

ALL: BLESSED ARE YOU, GOD OUR PASSIONATE LIFE

Leader: But if we have forgotten those who bear the marks of
exile, desert, home, upon their hands and feet
and suffer them to go on bleeding
if we have dismembered the body of God

ALL: HAVE MERCY ON US, GOD WHO BRINGS US
DOWN TO EARTH
GROUND US IN JUSTICE
ROOT US IN RIGHT RELATIONSHIP
GIVE FLESH TO OUR WORDS AND WORSHIP

WITH THE BREATH AND PEACE OF YOUR SPIRIT
UNTIL JOY IS OUR ONLY HOLY, COMMON GROUND
AMEN

Readings

Luke 24, vs 13 - 35 ■ *John 15, vs 16-17*

Prayers of concern

- for all sick or grieving people
- for new or renewing communities and nations

Chant

THROUGH OUR LIVES AND BY OUR PRAYERS
YOUR KINGDOM COME

- for those caught up in war or violence
- for those who are especially dear to us
- for co-operative relationship with the earth,
  and one another

Closing responses

Leader: Look at your hands
See the touch and the tenderness
ALL: GOD'S OWN FOR THE WORLD

Leader: Look at your feet
See the path and the direction
ALL: GOD'S OWN FOR THE WORLD

Leader: Look at your heart
See the fire and the love
ALL: GOD'S OWN FOR THE WORLD

Leader: Look at the cross
See God's Son and our Saviour
ALL: GOD'S OWN FOR THE WORLD
Leader: This is God's world
ALL: WE WILL SERVE GOD IN IT
AMEN [3]

Leaving song

Halleluiah we sing your praises ■ *Jesus Christ is waiting*
Amen Alleluia ■ *For yours is the kingdom* ■ *Behold I make*
all things new

People may go out singing, since the journey goes on.
Alternatively, the liturgy may end with a joyful
acclamation, a **Gloria** *or* **Alleluia***.*

| 8 | *Local church pilgrimage* |

Many churches have anniversaries, patronal festivals and dedication services which can be enhanced by a time spent remembering places of particular importance in the church building and celebrating what such places evoke.

In larger churches, it may be possible to physically move the congregation around the building in procession, singing an appropriate song or chant as they move from one venue to another. (Remember that people on the move cannot read words easily, so it's better to have a repetitive song which may range from a simple **Gloria** *to* **We Are Marching In The Light Of God***).*

In smaller churches, it may be sufficient either for the worship leader to move from one place to another, or to have different leaders who stand at the various places of significance.

What is said at each place may range from a reminder of its importance following the song, to personal testimonies from different people at each location followed by shared corporate prayer.

This type of pilgrimage was originally used in a very large Anglican church in Leeds, where 120 people walked through the building and into the halls. It has also been used in small Methodist chapels.

The first thing is to identify places of significance.

Here are some:

The door
Where some people enter and others pass by.

The font
The place of common entry into the community of the church.

The crossing
(Or altar steps, etc.) where people take vows of marriage.

The pulpit
From which successive preachers have proclaimed the Word of God.

The table or altar
Where Christ is host and which links us with the church in heaven.

The noticeboard
Which reminds us of the range of activities which happen in the church.

The kitchen
Where people, often unthanked, prepare food (and which may be a place of cooking for a soup-run, etc).

Here are examples of what might be said at two such places:

The door
'This is the door through which we enter church on Sundays. It is also the door past which many walk, some of whom have been turned away from faith by the unwelcoming or judgemental nature of churches they once went to.

Let us pray for people who we dearly wish would find their way into the church, saying their first names aloud if any so wish.'

(Names ... silence ... chant/song)

The altar/table

'This is the communion table where Jesus Christ invites us to share in a meal where he is host. This is the table around which generations of people have gathered. So here we may remember those who once sat with us at God's table on earth, and now sit at God's table in heaven, and in gratitude we name them.'

(Names ... silence ... chant/song)

Even if the Pilgrimage is going to move people around the building, it is good to have different people involved at each place of significance. To simplify matters, one person might lead the way and enable the prayer, while others say words which they have devised, appropriate to the various locations.

Chant(s)

The Door: *Here I stand at the door and knock* • **The Font:** *Pour out, I will pour out* • **The Crossing:** *Gloria* • **The Pulpit:** *Deus de Deo* • **The Table:** *Behold the Lamb of God* • **The Noticeboard:** *Kumbaya* • **The Kitchen:** *Let the giving of thanks*

Healing

Since its beginning, the ministry of healing has played a vital and central part in the life of the Iona Community. We believe in the integrity of creation: ... 'and God saw that it was very good.' We believe that this integrity, broken by sin, has been restored in Jesus Christ, that we are called to recognise it and to realise it, to live undivided lives, and to work for the healing of divisions wherever we encounter them. The healing of broken bodies, divided communities and nations, the healing of the earth itself, and our relationship with it, are all part of the integrity to which God calls us. They are all part of the ministry of healing.

Therefore, it is a ministry in which justice is as important as medicine; in which reverence for the earth (which may show up as recycling ... or just cycling) is as important as respect for the person suffering from mental illness; in which the health of the body politic matters as much as the health of the body personal. Indeed, they are inextricably linked. George MacLeod used to say, 'It is blasphemous to pray for Margaret with bronchitis, if we are not prepared to do something about the damp housing which causes her bronchitis.'

The ministry of healing is not only an exterior one. We are also invited to the healing of the divisions and splits in our own lives —the separation of the spiritual and the material is simply not possible if we believe that Jesus really lived in the flesh, was

Incarnate, made holy/whole the human body. So we cannot separate our actions from their consequences, our freedom from our responsibility, our lives as individuals from our lives as persons in community. We are invited into the community of God.

This community, we believe, extends over the limitations of time and space. We are part of the communion of saints, our wholeness is inclusive, not exclusive. Even in death, we are not divided ...

The three liturgies in this section include one of prayers for healing, including the laying on of hands; a liturgy for laying down and letting go of what has been in order to move into a greater wholeness; and a liturgy of thanksgiving for the communion of saints.

Notes on prayers for healing

A service of prayer for healing gives an opportunity to pray for individuals and communities who are in need, and also for those present to share in and receive the ministry of the laying on of hands. The way the service is organised will need to be sensitive to the experience and tradition of both worshippers and worship leaders. The following are a few notes for guidance, both theological and practical.

A   The ministry of healing is not something to be practised in secret or to be limited to particular individuals. It is the work of the whole Christian community, and is as much a part of the Christian life as prayer and service.

B   The New Testament evidence is that both Jesus and the Christian community prayed for the sick and laid hands on them when they prayed. We know in our daily lives that it is often touch, the hand on the shoulder, the hug of a friend, the cuddle of a child, that lets us know that we are loved. Touch, often more than words, is a way of giving physical expression to our prayers and concerns for each other.

C   Christian healing is about wholeness. Sickness is not limited to physical inability. Our past experience of hurt, our tangled emotions and our inability to forgive or be forgiven, all make us less than whole, and in need of healing.

D   The prayer for healing is about communities as well as individuals. Justice and healing walk hand-in-hand. The things which cause people to be hurt sometimes require a political solution arising out of our prayer. Our worship and our daily lives belong together.

E   To be involved in the healing ministry requires our willingness to be involved in the process of change. We may find ourselves called to listen, to visit, to support, to forgive. We may find ourselves involved in social and political action that will not only challenge the way things are, but that will challenge our attitudes and values as well.

F   The healing ministry is a shared ministry. The healer is God, who makes us whole, and can use each one of us, broken as we are, to express God's healing and love. It is appropriate that people should, if they choose, both receive and take part in ministry, and it is appropriate to invite people to do so.

G   A short repeated prayer accompanying the laying on of hands enables the whole congregation to focus on what is happening.

H   If possible, the laying on of hands should take place in the midst of the congregation, so that everyone is as much involved as possible.

I   People and communities are prayed for by name, because each person and situation is known to God, not as a problem to be solved, but as people who are accepted and understood and loved. We trust God to answer our prayers for healing, but we do not know how or when healing will happen. We trust God to act in love.

J Praying for healing is in no sense a rejection of the work of medicine, which is also a gift of God. Prayer is not an alternative but a complement to other forms of healing, and a recognition that healing comes in many ways, and is in essence concerned with wholeness and not simply cure.

9 *Brokenness and wholeness: a service of prayers for healing*

Opening responses

Leader: We come in worship to God
ALL: IN OUR NEED, AND BRINGING WITH US
THE NEEDS OF THE WORLD
Leader: We come to God, who comes to us in Jesus
ALL: AND WHO KNOWS BY EXPERIENCE
WHAT HUMAN LIFE IS LIKE
Leader: We come with our faith and with our doubts
ALL: WE COME WITH OUR HOPES
AND WITH OUR FEARS
Leader: We come as we are, because it is God
who invites us to come
ALL: AND GOD HAS PROMISED NEVER
TO TURN US AWAY

Song

Jesus Christ is Waiting ■ We Lay Our Broken World ■
Out of our failure to create ■ Those Who Wait on the Lord

Prayers of approach and confession

We are here, God
We have felt your touch in the sunlight
seen your power in the salt waves.
We have wondered at your mystery in the stars
and we marvel that the maker of the universe
knows us by name
We are here, God.
WE ARE HERE TO PRAISE AND WORSHIP YOU

We are here, Jesus
We know that you came to find us,
We have listened to your words
and smiled at your stories.
We have felt the warmth of your love, and
we thank you that you have called us friends.
We are here, Jesus.
WE ARE HERE TO PRAISE AND WORSHIP YOU

We are here, Holy Spirit
We are grateful for your presence
grateful for the way you bring us close —
for the way you comfort us and challenge us
and keep us right.
We are here, Holy Spirit.
WE ARE HERE TO PRAISE AND WORSHIP YOU.

We are here, God
In this moment, in this place
and we thank you that you are here with us.

You know us, God
We do not have to pretend with you.

In the silence of your love, we bring you
the things that trouble us
that harm us
that make us feel ashamed or afraid
Silence
God have mercy on us
CHRIST HAVE MERCY ON US
God have mercy on us
Silence
Listen to the words of Jesus,
words that we can trust:
'Don't be afraid

Your sins are forgiven
I love you
Come and follow me.'
Thanks be to God.
AMEN

Readings

Song

We Cannot Measure How You Heal ■ *A Touching Place*
Lay your hands gently upon us ■ *Take This Moment* ■
When our Lord walked the earth

Prayers of intercession

Please feel free to name places and names in the silences
We are your people, God
In this time and place,
you have called us to pray for those in need

We pray for the people whose names the world knows,
whose stories are told daily in the news ...
Silence
God in your mercy
HEAR OUR PRAYER

We pray for people in places of suffering,
whose names only you and their friends
and families know,
and whose lives you cherish ...
Silence
God in your mercy
HEAR OUR PRAYER

We pray for the people whose names and lives we
know, those who today are in pain or distress or
trouble,
those who are happy, those who are sad ...
Silence
God in your mercy
HEAR OUR PRAYER

We pray for ourselves, God
You know each one of us by name.
Make us into the people you want us to be,
and when that hurts,
reassure us how much you love us.
God, we bring you ourselves and our prayers
in Jesus' name
AMEN

Prayer for the laying on of hands

Those present who wish to receive the laying on of
hands are invited to take a place at kneelers or chairs
set out in a circle. Those who wish to share in this
ministry should also come and stand behind those
kneeling or sitting. In turn, hands are laid on the head
or shoulders of those who kneel or sit. They may then
move back to allow others to take a place.

It is quite appropriate both to receive and to share in
the laying on of hands if so wished.

SPIRIT OF THE LIVING GOD,
PRESENT WITH US NOW
ENTER YOU, BODY, MIND AND SPIRIT,
AND HEAL YOU OF ALL THAT HARMS YOU,
IN JESUS' NAME, AMEN.

Closing prayer

Watch now, dear Lord,
with those who wake or watch or weep tonight,
and give your angels charge over those who sleep.
Tend your sick ones, O Lord Christ,
rest your weary ones,
bless your dying ones, soothe your suffering ones,
pity your afflicted ones, shield your joyous ones,
and all for your love's sake. (*St Augustine*)
AMEN

Closing responses

Leader: For loving the world and knowing our names
          thank you God
ALL: THANK YOU GOD

Leader: For your strength that fills us
          and your love that heals us
          thank you God
ALL: THANK YOU GOD

Leader: For your presence here with us today
          and for your hand that leads us into tomorrow
          thank you God
ALL: THANK YOU GOD

Leader: Come bless us, hold us, wrestle with us
          warm us in your embrace
ALL: FOR WE ARE YOUR PEOPLE
          AND YOU ARE OUR JUSTICE AND JOY
          AMEN

If this liturgy is to be part of a service of Holy Communion, the service may continue after the closing prayer with the Preparation of the Gifts/Peace.

| 10 | *A liturgy for laying down and letting go* |

This liturgy is appropriate for sad times and situations of ending, leaving, or departing; perhaps for leaving a job or moving house, or even moving to a new country; perhaps for the ending of a relationship; perhaps for a member of a family or community moving on. Sensitive care should be taken about the location of the liturgy, which should have meaning and significance for the person or persons involved.

As Columba laid down his books
and the security of a monastery
SO WE LAY DOWN WHAT IS PAST
AND LOOK TO THE FUTURE

As Aidan and Cuthbert let go
and travelled hopefully on
SO WE LET GO HURT AND PAIN
AND TRAVEL WITH HOPE

As Hilda changed direction
and relinquished cherished plans
SO WE LEAVE BEHIND FAMILIAR PATHS
AND TAKE NEW STEPS INTO THE UNKNOWN

Song

Prayer of confession
Merciful God,
for the things we have done that we regret,
forgive us;
for the things we have failed to do that we regret,
forgive us;
for all the times we have acted without love,
forgive us;
for all the times we have reacted without thought,
forgive us;

for all the times we have withdrawn care,
forgive us;
for all the times we have failed to forgive,
forgive us.

For hurtful words said and helpful words unsaid,
for unfinished tasks
and unfulfilled hopes,
God of all time
forgive us
and help us
to lay down our burden of regret.

An act of contrition

People may write what they wish to lay down on a piece of paper, distributed beforehand, and place it at the foot of a cross, or in a boat [coracle] or a rubbish bin, and where appropriate these may be carried out, launched forth or burnt.
Alternatively people could be invited to place a lit candle by a symbol of new beginnings [e.g., a sandal, keys, an A to Z, a book open on a fresh page].
It may be helpful to invite people to sow seeds of hope in a central pot, or sow individual ones, reminding them that we can't sow seeds with a closed hand.

Dandelion clock

Hope is a dark elusive child
curled in the womb
cradled in our arms.
It can be lost,
disappear,
blown on the wind like a dandelion clock.

Its going,
its ebbing away
leaves us
grieving,
empty,
hopeless.

'But' is a hopeful word.

But even as the gossamer
powder puff
disintegrates,
the seeds are carried
to cling to distant crevices.
As it recedes
it reseeds
to grow again.

God, giver of peace,
grow hope within and around us.
God of steadfast love,
never leave us hopeless.

A time of silence for reflection

Litany of letting go

I let go:
window and door
house and home
memory and fear.
I let go the hurt of the past
and look to the hope of the future.
I let go
knowing that I will always carry
part of my past (part of you) with me
woven into the story of my life.

Help me/us, Christ my/our brother
to softly fold inside
the grief and the sadness,
to pack away the pain
and to move on;
taking each day in your company;
travelling each step
in your love.

To finish

Pilgrim God,
our shoes are filled with stones,
our feet are blistered and bleeding,
our faces are stained with tears.

As we stumble and fall
may we know your presence
in the bleeding and the tears
and in the healing and the laughter
of our pilgrimage.

11   *A liturgy for the communion of saints*

*Ideally, worship should happen in a circle, with space in the centre
for people to move back and forward. A cross should be placed in
the middle of the floor and around it should stand four candles.
Four objects are required to signify four stages of life. These might be:*

birth and infancy	—	*a rattle*
childhood	—	*a teddy bear*
adolescence	—	*a CD, cassette, record or school tie*
adulthood	—	*a set of keys*

*These should be in the possession of one person who will lay them
out at the appropriate time. Everyone should also have, if possible, a pencil or pen.*

*Everyone should be given an order of worship to which is stapled
four triangles encompassing three circles. This is an ancient Celtic
sign for a saint, sometimes found on the sleeves or hems of ancient
garments.*

*It is best if the worship takes place with dimmed lighting. The
liturgy should be led by a number of people. There is no need for
one voice or person to monopolise the parts. But it would be
helpful if someone ran over the order and rehearsed unknown
songs before worship begins.*

Opening reading

Reader: Bright, bright
The fellowship of saints in light,
Far, far beyond all earthly sight.
No plague can blight, no foe destroy.
United here they live in love:
O then above how deep their joy.

Set free
By Jesu's mortal wounds are we,
Blest with rich gifts — and more shall be.
Blessings has he in endless store:
Some drops are showered upon us here:
What when he hear the ocean's roar. [1]

or

Reader: Snivelling Zaccheus, fiddler of books,
Hated by all but his fraternal crooks;
Blind Bartimaeus, unkeen to keep silence
Shouts from his bench in the beggar's alliance.

Thomas the cynic, the seeker of proof,
Doubts eyewitness stories and keeps quite aloof;
And shy Nicodemus, avoiding daylight,
Prefers anonymity granted by night.

A well-seasoned widow, alone at a well,
With four or five husbands, if only she'd tell;
A Roman centurion, proud of his power,
Confronts his own weakness in death's fatal hour.

And Martha and Mary, both numbed by their grief,
Unable to cope or find hope in belief;
And James and John, brothers, beloved by their mum,
Obsessed by their seats in the kingdom to come;

And Peter with loyalty left in the lurch.
What a risk! —
'It is on this rock, I'll build my church.'

Song

From Erin's shores Columba came ■ *The strangest of saints*

Prayer A

Leader: O High King of Heaven,
In the early days, when the church was young,
You called, in the wake of the apostles,
Princes and common folk to carry the Gospel
To unbelieving lands.
Thus Patrick and Columba, Bride and Aidan
Nurtured communities of faith
On these and other shores.

ALL: FOR THEM AND FOR ALL ANCIENT SAINTS
WHO BROUGHT CHRIST'S WORD TO CELTIC
LANDS
WE PRAISE YOU;
AND ASK THAT IN THESE LATER DAYS
THE ZEAL OF EARLY PIONEERS
MAY STILL INFUSE YOUR CHURCH
AMEN
or

Prayer B

Leader: Lord Jesus Christ,
You built your church on the rock of
redeemed humanity;
Through Peter and Paul,
through Columba and Margaret,
through Luther, Teresa, John 23rd, Bonhoeffer,
through all the saints of every age,
you extended, reformed
and diversified the household of faith.

ALL: WE, WHO INHERIT THEIR WORK TODAY
AND REAP FROM WHAT OTHERS HAVE SOWN,
BLESS YOU FOR ALL OUR MOTHERS AND FATHERS
IN GOD.
LIKE THEM, MAY WE SO LOVE AND SERVE
YOUR KINGDOM
THAT GENERATIONS YET UNBORN
MAY BENEFIT FROM OUR WITNESS;
AND, WHEN THE GRACE OF LIFE ON EARTH
SHALL END,
FIND FOR US A PLACE
IN THE COMPANY OF HEAVEN,
FOR YOUR LOVE'S SAKE
AMEN

Words from the Saints

*These or other short passages may be used, of which the
first should be biblical*

Reader 1: A Word from St Paul:
Be always humble, gentle and patient.
Show your love by being tolerant to one another.
Do your best to preserve the unity
which the Spirit gives you
by means of the peace which binds you together.
There is one body.
There is one Spirit.
There is one hope
to which God has called his saints.

Reader 2: A Word from St Teresa:
Be careful lest praise from others harms you,
especially when people tell you that you are
more saintly than others,
Remember how John the Baptist was extolled
then beheaded;
and how our Lord was praised on Palm Sunday
then derided on Good Friday.

Struggle with your own heart
against dangerous flattery.

Reader 3: A Word from St Francis:
Our place is to be with the suffering,
the lepers, the starving.
In the depths of their hearts,
as in the hearts of even the saintliest person
there sleeps a horrible, unclean larva.
Lean over it and say to this larva, 'I love you'
and it will sprout wings and become like a butterfly.
O God of love, we bow to your power.
Come and kiss us, and accomplish your miracle.

Song

Ipharadisi

Meditation

Those whose lives touched ours
*Four people should read this meditation, each section
being preceded by the singing of the chant, during
which the person who has the four symbols lays them,
one at a time, beside a candle. It may be that during
the meditation, participants might want to write the
name of someone who comes to mind on one of the
triangles of paper.*
*After all the sections have been read, and all the sym-
bols are out, the chant is sung repeatedly as people place
their 'saints' beside the appropriate symbols.*

Chant

UBI CARITAS ET AMOR
UBI CARITAS, DEUS IBI EST.
(*"Where there is love and caring, God is there"*)
or

I AM THE VINE AND YOU THE BRANCHES
PRUNED AND PREPARED FOR ALL TO SEE,
READY TO BEAR THE FRUIT OF HEAVEN
IF YOU BELIEVE AND TRUST IN ME.

First symbol is placed

Voice 1:   Before I was born,
           you prayed for me;
           and when I moved from the womb to the world,
           your arms cradled me;
           and you sang funny songs,
           and you made sense of my gurgling language,
           and you held my hand till I slept,
           till I walked,
           till I lost my fear,
           till I was old enough to let your hand go.

Chant

Second symbol is placed

Voice 2:   When I was young,
           you prayed for me;
           when I broke my heart or bruised my skin,
           you cared for me;
           when I was keen to learn,
           you taught me;
           you watched my eyes bulge
           with the wonder of the world.
           You heard me repeat you;
           you let me cheat you;
           you often said yes and sometimes said no.
           And even today,
           I am enriched and restrained
           by what you did then.

Chant

Third symbol is placed

Voice 3:   When I left childhood,
you prayed for me;
when I was stubborn with my parents,
I could talk to you;
when I felt awkward with my body,
I felt comfortable with you.
And though you gave me good advice,
you saw me ignore it;
and though you gave me liberty,
you saw me abuse it;
and though you spoke of God,
you saw I did not want to know;
but still you held me through the difficult days
and I reap the benefit now.

Chant

Fourth symbol is placed

Voice 4:   Since I've become the adult
that I longed to be,
you've prayed for me;
when I had to cope with my failures,
you've accepted me;
when I was unsure of myself,
you've believed in me;
when I've stood on the brink of decisions,
you've stood beside me;
and when doubts had their day
and faith seemed remote
and the church irrelevant,
you've let God touch me.

Chant

Sung repeatedly as triangles are placed near appropriate symbols.
Silence

Closing song

O God, thou art the Father ■ *For all the saints who've shown your love*

Blessing

The leader begins and thereafter people may add words as appropriate after which all share the response. The leader concludes with final sentence.

Leader: The God of Abraham and Sarah
ALL: STAY WITH US NOW
Leader: The God of Moses and Elijah
ALL: STAY WITH US NOW
Leader: The God of Andrew, Peter, James and John
ALL: STAY WITH US NOW
Leader: The God of Mary of Magdala
ALL: STAY WITH US NOW

Other names, biblical or otherwise may be added here

Leader: The God of our Lord and Saviour Jesus Christ,
          crucified, dead, risen and ascended,
          keep us in the commonwealth of heaven
          now and evermore.
ALL: AMEN

1   Taken from *Threshold of Light*, edited by Esther de Waal and AM Allchin published and copyright 1986 by Darton, Longman and Todd Ltd and used by permission of the publishers

Acts of witness and dissent

The Rule of the Iona Community commits its members to action for justice and peace in society. Our Justice and Peace Commitment, which is a 'point of departure' rather than final destination, has, as its sixth point, the belief that '… social and political action leading to justice for all people, and encouraged by prayer and discussion, is a vital work of the church at all levels,' and, as its eighth point, the commitment to '… engage in forms of political witness and action, prayerfully and thoughtfully, to promote just and peaceful social, political and economic structures.' It is as a basic tenet of faith that members of the Iona Community engage in political activity, rather than attachment to any particular political agenda.

But our engagement is constantly driving us into prayer. As George MacLeod, the founder of the Community, wrote, 'There are evenings when our prayer life is refreshing: but analysed, they turn out to be the times when the pressures have been so weighty that you have simply had to go with them to God. But this is precisely the recovery of the knife-edge. The religious moment flowers from the practical.' Nowhere is this more true than on the knife-edge of political and social engagement.

Many of the most significant acts of worship for members of the Community on the mainland have not been in churches.

They have been outdoors, on demonstrations and marches and picket-lines, outside military bases and the Ministry of Defence, in city squares and at embassies. Equally importantly, though perhaps less dramatically, they have been in homes and community centres, in schools and factories and hospitals, all the places where people struggle on a knife-edge and we among them. At the very least, we can take our bodies, and our prayers, and say with them, 'I beg to differ', we can witness to our conviction that 'it is better to light a candle than to curse the darkness.'

Erik Cramb, a member of the Community who is an industrial chaplain on Tayside, wrote about his involvement on the picket line in the Timex dispute in Dundee:

> 'We can stand on the sidelines and roundly condemn the attempts of Timex to force down wages in Dundee, and so we should. But we cannot pretend we're clean, we cannot pretend it's nothing to do with us. Those who seek to maximise our pension funds and our endowment policies are among the casino's biggest players ... Greed, timidity, dishonesty, hopelessness, tears, exploitation, manipulation, violence, anger, betrayal, denial, decency, loyalty, unity, humour, forgiveness, generosity, solidarity ... all the great themes of the faith were there for anyone who had eyes to see and ears to hear. The hope of new life beyond the current turmoil was never entirely lost ... buds of faithfulness, of redemption ever present. To stand on the picket line was to be in the touching place, in the learning place, in the expectant place, to be where sin was, and was confronted by something better. Thank God, I was there!'

12 | Witness for peace :
celebration of life in death

A peace liturgy adapted from a service held at Faslane Trident Submarine Base on 27 October 1986

Introduction

Voice 1:   I looked at the earth — it was a barren waste; at the sky — there was no light. I looked at the mountains — they were shaking, and the hills were rocking to and fro. I saw that there were no people; even the birds had flown away. The fertile land had become a desert and its cities were in ruins.

Voice 2:   *Reading from Deuteronomy 30, vs 19*

Facing and naming the powers of death

A brief explanation is given of what goes on at this particular military establishment, and its destructive power.

All stand in silence for two minutes facing the powers

Song
By the Waters of Babylon

Prayer of repentance

in which we acknowledge our own complicity in the forces of death

Leader: Forgive us, Creator God,
          for we have seen into the abyss and not drawn back
          We pray for those of us who have the political power
          to make life or death decisions
ALL: WE HAVE SEEN INTO THE ABYSS
          AND NOT DRAWN BACK
SUNG: KYRIE ELEISON

Leader: We pray for those of us who can see no choice
          but to work in the industries of death
ALL: WE HAVE SEEN INTO THE ABYSS
          AND NOT DRAWN BACK
          KYRIE ELEISON

Leader: We pray for those of us who pay our taxes or make
          our profits out of the industries of death
ALL: WE HAVE SEEN INTO THE ABYSS
          AND NOT DRAWN BACK
          KYRIE ELEISON

Leader: We pray for those of us who have failed to speak
          loudly enough or take action boldly enough to chal-
          lenge the industries of death
ALL: WE HAVE SEEN INTO THE ABYSS
          AND NOT DRAWN BACK
          KYRIE ELEISON

Leader: We pray for those of us who have been too confused
          or helpless to know what to do
ALL: WE HAVE SEEN INTO THE ABYSS
          AND NOT DRAWN BACK
          KYRIE ELEISON

Leader: We know that with you life is abundant, and that you
          can make all things new
ALL: WE REJOICE IN YOUR HOPE

Reading

Romans 8, vs 35-39

Leader: Who shall separate us from the love of Christ
ALL: LET US CELEBRATE HOPE
IN THE VIBRANT LIFE OF CHRIST

Song

Those who wait on the Lord

Commitment to life

Leader: In the midst of hunger and war
ALL: WE CELEBRATE THE PROMISE
OF PLENTY AND PEACE

Leader: In the midst of oppression and tyranny
ALL: WE CELEBRATE THE PROMISE
OF SERVICE AND FREEDOM

Leader: In the midst of doubt and despair
ALL: WE CELEBRATE THE PROMISE
OF FAITH AND HOPE

Leader: In the midst of fear and betrayal
ALL: WE CELEBRATE THE PROMISE
OF JOY AND LOYALTY

Leader: In the midst of hatred and death
ALL: WE CELEBRATE THE PROMISE
OF LOVE AND LIFE

Leader: In the midst of sin and decay
ALL: WE CELEBRATE THE PROMISE
OF SALVATION AND RENEWAL

Leader: In the midst of death on every side
ALL: WE CELEBRATE THE PROMISE
OF THE LIVING CHRIST [1]

Words of encouragement

Reader: To do and dare — not what you would, but what is
right. Never to hesitate over what is in your power,
but boldly to grasp what lies before you. Not in the
flight of fancy, but only in the deed there is freedom.

Away with timidity and reluctance! Out into the
storm of event, sustained only by the commandment
of God and your faith, and freedom will receive your
spirit with exultation.
Dietrich Bonhoeffer [2]

or

Prayer for strength (spoken)

Leader: Lord, we do not pray for easy lives,
          we pray to be stronger people.
          We do not pray for tasks equal to our powers,
          but for powers equal to our tasks.
ALL: WE STAND TOGETHER FOR LIFE
          IN THE MIDST OF DEATH

Song

Be Not Afraid ■ *God Give Us Power* ■ *Sent by the Lord* ■
Oh Lord, Hold My Hand

Act of witness

During the singing, those who wish to make a particu-
lar witness for peace come forward. Actions can range
from lighting a candle for those who have inspired us,
to symbolic burning of missiles, to acts of civil disobedience.

Blessing

Leader: Go forth into the world in peace; be of good courage;
          hold fast that which is good; render to no one evil for
          evil; strengthen the fainthearted; support the weak;
          help the afflicted; honour all people; love and serve the
          Lord, rejoicing in the power of the Holy Spirit.
ALL: AMEN [3]

or

Leader: Sisters and brothers arise.
           Arise and lift your hearts, arise and lift your eyes
           arise and lift your voices.
           The living God, the living, moving Spirit of God
           sends us out together in witness
           in celebration
           in struggle
           reach out towards each other
           our God reaches out towards us [4]

1   Attributed to Edmund Jones. Reproduced by permission of
     Stainer & Bell
2   Dietrich Bonhoeffer, *Letters & Papers from Prison*,
     HarperCollins Publishers
3   Material from *The Prayer Book as Proposed in 1928* is
     copyright © The Central Board of Finance of the Church of
     England and is reproduced with permission
4   Elizabeth Rice, *No Longer Strangers; A Resource for Women
     and Worship*, edited by Iben Gjerding and Katherine
     Kinnamon © 1983 WCC Publications, World Council of
     Churches, Geneva, Switzerland.

13 | *Peace liturgy for a wet day*

As most demonstrations seem to take place in the pouring rain, this is a shortened version, in which no-one needs bits of paper which would otherwise get soggy.

Leader: *Reading from Deuteronomy 30, vs 19 ■ John 10, vs 10*
           An explanation is given about the base or military installation

           Song
           Kyrie Eleison
           Two-minute silence

Leader: We come to celebrate life

           Symbol of hope

           (Not a candle!) Plant a flower, name people who have inspired us, weave a rainbow with coloured threads, hand in a petition

           Prayer

           Hold hands and pray together: the Lord's Prayer, or the Prayer for Peace or have people share a story or sign of hope or keep silent
           After each one, all say:
           THE HOPE OF THE WORLD

           Song
           Amen Siyakadumiza ■ Allelujah ■ We Shall Overcome ■ We Are Marching in the Light of God

           Blessing

Leader: Let us share the Good News of peace in the world
           The peace of Christ be with you
ALL: AND ALSO WITH YOU

| 14 |

Cursing the 'money boys':
an act of witness for economic justice

The service begins with the congregation divided in two, facing each other. RHS and LHS indicate either side of the church, room, etc. The leader of worship stands in the middle.

Leader: Jesus said: Blessed are the comfortable,
         for God has shown them his favour
RHS: OH NO HE DIDN'T!
LHS: OH YES HE DID!

Leader: Jesus said: Blessed are those who have good pension
         funds, for God has shown them his favour
RHS: OH NO HE DIDN'T!
LHS: OH YES HE DID!

Leader: Jesus said: the strong and powerful
         will inherit the earth
RHS: OH NO HE DIDN'T!
LHS: OH YES HE DID!

Leader: Jesus said: Blessed are the winners,
         for they will inherit everything
RHS: OH NO HE DIDN'T!
LHS: OH YES HE DID!

Leader: Jesus said: Don't do anything to undermine the exist-
         ing order — to do so is to go against God
RHS: OH NO HE DIDN'T!
LHS: OH YES HE DID!

Leader: Jesus said: Look after yourself, then if you have
         something left over, give a coin to the poor
RHS: OH NO HE DIDN'T!
LHS: OH YES HE DID!

Leader: Jesus said: God is a nice old man,
           who doesn't want anyone to rock the boat
RHS: OH NO HE DIDN'T!
LHS: OH YES HE DID!

Reading
Matthew 21, vs 12-17

A member of the congregation narrates the story of the entry of Jesus into Jerusalem, which is enacted. Jesus strides down between the two groups and overturns the tables with a bang, scattering the money. The leader allows the uneasiness and the silence to grow.

Leader: Jesus said: Blessed are the poor in spirit,
           for the kingdom of God is theirs
ALL: KILL HIM!

Leader: Jesus said: How hard it is for those who have riches
           to enter the kingdom of heaven!
ALL: KILL HIM!

Leader: Jesus said: It is easier for a camel to go through
           the eye of a needle than it is for a rich man
           to enter the kingdom of heaven
ALL: KILL HIM!

Leader: Jesus said: Blessed are the meek,
           for they shall inherit the earth
ALL: KILL HIM!

Leader: Jesus said: Blessed are the peacemakers:
           they shall be called the children of God
ALL: KILL HIM!

Leader: Jesus said: Blessed are you when you suffer insults and
            persecutions and calumnies of every kind for my sake
ALL: KILL HIM!

Leader: Jesus said: Do not be anxious about tomorrow:
            tomorrow will look after itself
ALL: KILL HIM!

Leader: Jesus said: Alas for you who are rich:
            you have had your time of happiness!
ALL: KILL HIM!

Leader: Jesus said: Sell your possessions
            and give to the poor
ALL: KILL HIM!

Leader: Jesus said: Where your treasure is,
            there your heart will be also
ALL: KILL HIM!

Leader: Jesus said: Alas for you
            when all speak well of you!
ALL: KILL HIM!

Leader: Jesus said: If you want to be my disciple,
            you must take up your cross
            and follow me
ALL: KILL HIM! KILL HIM! KILL HIM!
            Silence

            *Reading of recent newspaper reports, read from differ-
            ent parts of the church: about the disparity between
            rich and poor; about Third World debt; about the role
            of world bankers. Then these words of George
            MacLeod's are introduced:*

Reader: Fifty years ago, George MacLeod, founder of the Iona
            Community, wrote these words:
            "Something must be done about the
            money boys who run our world. It is
            urgent that the whole issue of international
            monetary finance be reviewed.
            Have you ever queried the bankers? I
            have. Try the lower echelon of bankers, and
            most of them will say, 'These things are too
            high for us, we cannot attain unto them,'
            but a small minority will whisper, 'You've
            got something there, boy; isn't it extraordi-
            narily cold weather for so late in the month of
            May?'
            Try the upper echelon of bankers. I have.
            I wrote to the top man of a London bank, a
            charming man, asking his comments on a
            similar document to the Haslemere Decla-
            ration [*Declaration about world poverty*].
            He replied that the figures were inaccurate.
            I immediately asked which figures, but had
            no reply.
            They are in training for the job of interna-
            tional bankers. They know what is good for
            us. Don't consult us, the paltry crowd. But
            do they know what is good for us? Or are
            they sowing the seeds of the next war?" [1]

Song
For the Healing of the Nations (or another)

Readings
Psalms 24 ■ *Ephesians 6, vs 10-20*

Short meditation on the word

It should emphasise not only the global interlocking of the 'principalities and powers' which keep poor people in debt, but also individual attitudes to money.

Prayers of intercession

Song
Almighty Father of all things that be (or another)

Closing responses

Leader: We will not offer to the Lord
ALL: OFFERINGS THAT COST US NOTHING

Leader: Go in peace, to love and serve the Lord
ALL: WE WILL SEEK PEACE AND PURSUE IT

Leader: Glory be to the Father and to the Son
          and to the Holy Spirit
ALL: AS IT WAS IN THE BEGINNING, IS NOW AND
          EVER SHALL BE,
          WORLD WITHOUT END.
          AMEN

1   *George MacLeod*, Ron Ferguson, HarperCollins Publishers, p. 364, 1990

15   *Common ground:*
an act of witness against racism

This act of witness should take place with people seated in a circle or semicircle so that they can face each other with a space in the midst of them. It may be appropriate to hold it in a place that represents neutral ground for people of differing backgrounds and faiths, e.g. a school, community centre, etc.

Voice 1:   *Listen to the words of a British Asian woman:*
'We are told that human rights law is about uniting families. But Asian people see regularly that Britain's immigration laws are separating families. After three years waiting, I am completely sickened and worn out by the delay and the worry. As British citizens, we have no right to family life. Yet women in Europe may enter Britain with husbands, children and entire family without application, without interviews. There will be no racial justice for us until the law is changed. The politicians have failed us. People of faith must give a lead.'
From a statement made by a Muslim woman in Manchester Cathedral on Human Rights Day 1989, before an audience of Muslims, Sikhs, Hindus, Jews and Christians.

Leader: A welcome to you all.
Some of us have strong faith. In some of us, faith falters.
But we are all here as children of God,
as inhabitants of one earth.
We bring to this place our fears and anxieties,
our visions and dreams for the future.
We bring our politics and our prayers,
our strengths and our weaknesses,
our issues and our concerns,

and we lay them out on the ground,
hoping that the middle ground may become,
not wasteground,
not battleground,
but common ground.

People may, at this point, bring out symbols or placards representing some of their concerns, e.g. a passport, no entry signs, and lay them in the space or on a table in the middle.

Song of hope and solidarity
He Came Down ■ Let's Walk Together ■ Come Now, O Prince of Peace ■ If You Believe and I Believe

Voice 2:   Listen to these words from the World Council of Churches: 'Every human being, created in the image of God, is a person for whom Christ has died. Racism, which is the use of a person's racial origins to determine the person's value, is an assault on Christ's value and a rejection of his sacrifice.'[1]

Voice 3:   Listen to these words from Matthew 23, vs 23: Jesus said: How terrible for you, teachers of the Law and Pharisees! You hypocrites! You give God a tenth even of the seasoning herbs such as mint, dill and cumin, but you neglect to obey the really important teachings of the law, such as justice and mercy and honesty.[2]

Prayers for forgiveness

Leader: Helder Camara said that
it is very difficult to create awareness
in the privileged.

LET US PRAY
God, you call us to see and hear and understand,
to open our eyes and ears and hearts,
to be aware,
forgive us for our false pride and complacency
for our unthinking consumerism

ALL: LORD HAVE MERCY UPON US

Leader: Forgive us for our insularity
for our reluctance to accept new ways

ALL: LORD HAVE MERCY UPON US

Leader: Forgive us for our complaining,
for growing bitter and sorry for ourselves,
for becoming hardened and indifferent
to the pain of others

ALL: LORD HAVE MERCY UPON US

Voice 1: 'Why do you treat Asian people like this? Don't you
understand that Jesus was an Asian? Would you do
this to Jesus?'
*(A Muslim woman, angry at the treatment of
Asian families under UK immigration laws)*
Silence

Leader: God, make us aware, make us repentant,
we turn to you,
heal us of our privileged blindness,
and make us whole.

ALL: AMEN

Sharing stories

People now have the opportunity to share their stories, in whatever form they wish to tell them, and to be heard without interruption or dismissal.

Sharing memories

People are now invited to share in a 'collective memory-making' in which a particular theme or issue, e.g. law, family, travel, are either written on a large sheet of paper or written on small pieces and collected in a basket. By 'remembering' different aspects of the same thing, a collective memory is created which is presented for prayer, and may be printed and used later.

During this time a song or chant may be sung.

Song or chant

Send out your light ■ *Word of the Father* ■ *Listen Lord* ■ *Come Holy Spirit*

Readings

Isaiah 58, vs 6 - 12 ■ *passages from the Koran and the Talmud may be used, as well as the Scriptures of other faiths*

Prayers of concern

During the prayers of concern, a candle may be lit after each petition and placed in the centre space, beside the symbols or placards of concern and the collective memory.

Leader: Come God,
        listen to the calling of those with nowhere to turn
        at the point where support fails,
        the majority turns away,
        and we/they are alone

ALL: WE CANNOT REMAIN SILENT
          BECAUSE WE FEAR THE AUTHORITIES
          AND DO NOT WANT TO ROCK THE BOAT [3]

Leader: We remember those who suffer
          as a result of family break-up
          or unjust immigration or nationality laws
ALL: WE CANNOT REMAIN SILENT
          BECAUSE WE FEAR THE AUTHORITIES
          AND DO NOT WANT TO ROCK THE BOAT

Leader: We remember those who suffer harassment or abuse
          in the street or school or workplace
          as a result of their religion or skin colour
ALL: WE CANNOT REMAIN SILENT
          BECAUSE WE FEAR THE AUTHORITIES
          AND DO NOT WANT TO ROCK THE BOAT

Leader: God of justice, give us voice, take away our fear, shake
          up our prejudices and move us to a different place, to
          stand on common ground with those who struggle for
          justice.
ALL: AMEN

Common ground statement

*People may be invited before the reading of this state-
ment on racism to leave their places and stand in the
centre space as a sign of solidarity with its intention*

Leader: RACISM IS A SIN AGAINST GOD
          AND AGAINST FELLOW HUMAN BEINGS.
          IT IS CONTRARY TO THE JUSTICE
          AND THE LOVE OF GOD.
          IT DESTROYS THE HUMAN DIGNITY
          OF BOTH THE RACIST AND THE VICTIM.
          WHEN PRACTISED, IT DENIES ANY FAITH
          OR CONVICTION WE PROFESS TO HOLD.
          WE CONDEMN RACISM IN ALL ITS FORMS.

Reading

Luke 4, vs 18-19

ALL: THE SPIRIT OF THE LORD IS UPON ME,
BECAUSE HE HAS CHOSEN ME
TO BRING GOOD NEWS TO THE POOR,
HE HAS SENT ME
TO PROCLAIM LIBERTY TO THE CAPTIVES
AND RECOVERY OF SIGHT TO THE BLIND,
TO SET FREE THE OPPRESSED,
AND ANNOUNCE THAT THE TIME HAS COME
WHEN THE LORD WILL SAVE HIS PEOPLE [4]

Song

Stand Firm

Closing prayer

Leader: God, lead us that we may stand firm in faith for justice.
ALL: TEACH US LOVE. TEACH US COMPASSION.
ABOVE ALL, OUT OF LOVE AND COMPASSION,
TEACH US TO ACT.
AMEN

1   World Council of Churches' Statement and Actions on
     Racism 1948 - 1979 © 1980 WCC Publications, World
     Council of Churches, Geneva, Switzerland
2   Scriptures quoted from the *Good News Bible* published by
     The Bible Societies/HarperCollins Publishers Ltd., UK ©
     American Bible Society, 1966, 1971, 1976, 1992, with
     permission
3   The Road to Damascus, CIIR/Christian Aid
4   Scriptures quoted from the *Good News Bible* published by
     The Bible Societies/HarperCollins Publishers, UK ©
     American Bible Society, 1966, 1971, 1976, 1992, with
     permission

A sanctuary and a light

The Prayer for the Iona Community (see *An Act of Prayer*) asks; '... if it be your holy will, grant that a place of your abiding be continued still to be a sanctuary and a light.' This is usually assumed to be a reference to the Community's residential centres on Iona and Mull, and yet the prayer is one for the Community, not the buildings. There is a sense in which the prayer can also be for the embodiment of these characteristics in the people.

They are, of course, first and foremost attributes of God, 'God our refuge and our strength', the Lord who is 'our light and our salvation', in whom we find the secure love, the safe place that all of us long for and need in order to be truly free; and yet who leads us on and out into the world, into challenge and adventure and discipleship. The movement of coming home and going out is a constant dynamic of faith; the two exist in a creative relationship in which each needs the other. Without the light that leads us out, our security becomes complacent and self-absorbed.

But without the sanctuary, the safe place of return (whether in our communities, our homes, or in our solitude with God), our activity becomes brittle, exhausted and often fearful.

The three liturgies here are all about right relationship of sanctuary and light; the first focusing on the experience of women, for whom it has often been a distorted relationship; the second is especially for children and adults to share, for whom a right relationship of sanctuary and light is a crucial part of life and faith nurture; and the third is an act of prayer for members of the Community when they gather.

| 16 | *Women: refuge and adventure*

*This liturgy was written for use in a Scottish context
[Thenew, also known as Enoch and mentioned later in
this liturgy, was the mother of St Mungo or Kentigern,
patron saint of Glasgow] but can be adapted for use in
other contexts, with the insertion of other names [a
fruitful and interesting area of research into the hidden
history of women in the church].*

Leader: Let us enter into the presence of God,
          God, Creator Spirit
          You are Breath
ALL: BREATHE NEW LIFE INTO US
Leader: You are Fire
ALL: INFLAME OUR COLDNESS WITH LOVE
Leader: You are Wind
ALL: LET US RIDE ON YOUR WHIRLING WINGS
Leader: You are Refuge
ALL: OUR SHELTER IS IN YOU

Song

The Love Burning Deep (or another)

Leader: Come and share the story of women. Let us listen to
          their voices, honour their lives, affirm their gifts, weep
          for their suffering, and celebrate their embodiment in
          the image of God
ALL: FOR THEIR VOICES ARE OUR VOICES
          THEIR BODIES ARE OUR BODIES
          THEIR STRUGGLES ARE OUR STRUGGLES
          AND WE SHARE A COMMON HUMANITY

Litany of violence

Voice 1:   I am Hagar, slavewoman banished to wander in the desert

Voice 1:   I am Tamar, raped by my brother and then reviled

Voice 1:   I am Jepthah's daughter — killed as an offering to God

Voice 1:   I am all the nameless, voiceless, forgotten ones

Leader: Women of the Bible, violated and abandoned,
where shall you find refuge?

ALL: OUT OF THE DEPTHS WE CRY TO YOU, GOD
HEAR OUR CRY AND LISTEN TO OUR PRAYER

Voice 1:   I am Thenew, a Christian convert, chased from my home
for refusing my father's choice of husband; raped in a
field; stoned and abused, twice sentenced to death;
homeless when my child was born

Leader: Mother of Mungo, hidden from history,
where shall you find refuge?

ALL: OUT OF THE DEPTHS WE CRY TO YOU, GOD
HEAR OUR CRY AND LISTEN TO OUR PRAYER

Voice 1:   I am four thousand Scottish women; persecuted,
tortured
and accused of witchcraft; stripped, strangled and
burned in a frenzy of terror

Leader: Women punished for being different,
where shall you find refuge?

ALL: OUT OF THE DEPTHS WE CRY TO YOU, GOD
HEAR OUR CRY AND LISTEN TO OUR PRAYER

Voice 1:   I am numberless women all over the world;
this day and every day, beaten and bloodied,
battered and bruised by the men they live with

Leader: Women, your home is where the hurt is
where shall you find refuge?

ALL: OUT OF THE DEPTHS WE CRY TO YOU, GOD
HEAR OUR CRY AND LISTEN TO OUR PRAYER

Silence, for reflection on these and others, known and unknown, who have been victims and survivors of violence

Leader: For too long we have worshipped a god of fear and anger
a god of injustice and exclusion
a god who values men more highly than women
a god who abandons us in our pain and sorrow.
Let us repent of all the harm done to women
in the name of that mean and dangerous god
and banish him from our hearts, our homes, our communities

SUNG: KYRIE ELEISON

Leader: Spirit of love, under your strong and tender wings there is refuge for all who are exploited, harassed, patronised, demeaned and abused. Shield, nurture and restore us to wholeness and integrity, in our personal and corporate lives. In your shelter, let us create a safe place to be ourselves, to explore new possibilities, to share friendship and to sustain each other in the struggle for liberation.
Amen.

Psalm 27

This can either be read responsively, or by one voice, or can be sung

Reading

Luke 8, vs 42b-48

Litany of empowerment

During this litany, candles are lit for each group of women honoured. In a small gathering, each person might take it in turn to read. The sections should be adapted and added to as appropriate for those present, and space given to invite participants to speak names, or share their own stories of women.

Leader: God, the refuge you offer is no hiding place from the world
It is a sanctuary for survivors, where you warm us with shared experience, and kindle in us a passion to struggle against cruelty, exclusion and oppression.
Your wings lift us high with hope and laughter. Soaring above loneliness and pain, we see a vision of what might be. So let us celebrate the adventure of women who act with courage and perception, to lighten our way.

Voice 4: This is the light of Ruth; a foreigner who journeyed into the unknown for the sake of love and loyalty to Naomi, and who acted with initiative to change their lives for the better
ALL: FOR THIS WE PRAISE YOU,
AND CLAIM RUTH'S POWER OF SOLIDARITY

Voice 4: This is the light of Joanna and Susanna, who knew and loved Jesus,
who comforted, challenged and inspired his ministry,
who witnessed a new way of living
ALL: FOR THIS WE PRAISE YOU,
AND CLAIM THE DISCIPLES' POWER
OF COMMITMENT

Voice 4: This is the light of Thenew, who was resolute in faith, and prevailed against the worst men could do, to find a safe home for herself and her child

ALL: FOR THIS WE PRAISE YOU,
AND CLAIM THENEW'S POWER
TO OVERCOME ADVERSITY

Voice 4: This is the light of Celtic women, who integrated action and contemplation, passion for creation with respect for learning

ALL: FOR THIS WE PRAISE YOU
AND CLAIM THE CELTIC POWER
OF ROOTED WISDOM

Voice: This is the light of women carers, nurses, midwives and doctors, present with compassion, expertise and humour throughout the cycle of life and death

ALL: FOR THIS WE PRAISE YOU
AND CLAIM THE HEALERS' POWER
OF TOUCH

Voice: This is the light of women who have struggled to build bridges of hope, justice and reconciliation in a world of poverty, suspicion and war; as peacemakers, politicians, community campaigners and good neighbours

ALL: FOR THIS WE PRAISE YOU,
AND CLAIM THE ACTIVISTS' POWER
TO DREAM DREAMS

Voice: This is the light of women who have shattered the silence of violence, by speaking out in the face of indifference, and by offering places of safety in which fear is banished and self-esteem affirmed

ALL: FOR THIS WE PRAISE YOU
AND CLAIM THE COLLECTIVE POWER
OF RIGHTEOUS ANGER

Voice: This is the light of untold women's lives, shining through hardship, sustained in hope, cherished in tenderness, poured out in passion, glowing with glorious life-giving love. It is the light of our mothers and grandmothers, our sisters and daughters, our friends and partners and lovers. It is the light of refuge and adventure

All join hands for blessing

ALL: FOR THIS WE PRAISE YOU,
AND BLESS EACH OTHER
AND CLAIM THE POWER OF WOMEN
TO LIVE IN FREEDOM, JUSTICE
AND WHOLENESS.
HALLELUJAH *(either as a song or a shout of acclamation)*

17 | *A safe place and a light: a liturgy for children and adults*

Opening responses

Leader: When we are happy
When we are full of fun and laughter
ALL: GOD WELCOMES US

Leader: When we are angry
When people let us down and make us sad
ALL: GOD WELCOMES US

Leader: When we are tired
When we need to stop and curl up and rest
ALL: GOD WELCOMES US

Leader: God of welcome
God whose door is always open
ALL: WE ARE GLAD TO MEET YOU HERE

Song

Heaven is singing for joy ■ *Halle, halle, halle* ■
Come host of heaven's high dwelling place ■
Amen Siakudumisa

The Word of God

Leader: Listen to God's Word. First we hear some words from the book of Zechariah that tells us about the sort of place God wants our world to be.

Then we'll listen to a child's retelling of the story of
Zacchaeus

Reader 1:   God gave this message to Zechariah
I have longed to help Jerusalem
because of my deep love for her people
I will return to Jerusalem and live there
It will be known as the faithful city.
Once again old men and women
so old that they use a stick when they walk
will be sitting in the city squares.
The streets will be full again
of boys and girls playing ...
people will sow their crops in peace
the vines will bear grapes
the earth will produce food
there will be plenty of rain ...

These are the things you must do
speak the truth to one another
in the courts give real justice
the kind that brings peace
do not plan ways to hurt each other
do not tell lies about each other.
Have courage
do not be afraid.
Love truth and love peace.

Reader 2:   One day there was a man called Zacchaeus. He was
working with his pen and paper. Zacchaeus said to the
people, 'Pay twelve coins.' He gave the Romans ten
coins and he kept two coins for himself and put it in
his pocket. So he was rich. He had a beautiful house.
One day Jesus came and Zacchaeus wanted to see him,
but he had one problem — he was little, so he could
not see over the people's heads. He saw a tree and
climbed up it. Jesus saw him and said, 'What are you

doing up there?' Everyone was laughing. Jesus said, 'Get down here Zacchaeus,' so he got down. Jesus said, 'I am coming up to yours for tea.' Zacchaeus was nervous — he got all his servants to tidy up — they got out all the best knives and forks and spoons and it all looked beautiful.

Jesus and Zacchaeus sat at the table and were talking. They drank all the wine and ate the food. Zacchaeus said, 'I am sorry about all of the things I have took off the poor people. I will give them their money back.' Jesus said, 'That's what I want to hear — you have got everything — sort it out.' Then they finished their tea.

Praying for ourselves

Voice 1:   Let us pray:
God, we live in a world that needs to change
we are part of the world
we do things that hurt each other
things that are wrong.
There are things that we need to sort out.

Silence to think about these things

ALL: GOD WE ARE SORRY
WE WANT TO DO THINGS DIFFERENTLY

Voice 2:   Let us listen to God's words
words for those who want to change.
In Jesus, God says to us:
'I know you are sorry
I forgive you
I love you
Don't be afraid'

ALL: GOD THANK YOU
THANK YOU FOR YOUR LOVE. AMEN.

Song

Take this moment, sign and space ■ *He came down*

Sharing our stories

Leader: For all of us it is important to know that we are loved, that people care for us and stand up for us. We need food to eat and safe places to sleep and work and play. For all of us, it is good to have places where we feel comfortable and safe, people we enjoy being with, and friends and family who love us. In a minute, can you get into groups of four or five people, maybe with people you don't know very well, and talk together about the places where you feel safe and the people you enjoy being with, and, if you've time, try and work out what makes those places feel safe and good. When you hear some music, it will be time to be quiet and come back to your seat. So go and talk together about the places and people that make you feel safe and good.

People get up and go to share their stories. Worship leaders may invite groups to share their findings with the congregation.

Praying for others

Leader: We are going to pray now for people around the world, who, like us, need to know that God loves them. We light candles as we pray, as a sign that God brings light and love into the world. After we have lit the first five larger candles, and when the music plays, you are invited to come and light a candle for anyone you know, or have heard about, who needs to know that God loves them.

Voice 1: We pray for the people of Africa
Add words for specific situation.

Someone brings a candle from the midst of the congregation and places it centrally, possibly on a map of the world.

Voice 2:   We pray for the people of the Americas
            (as Voice 1)

Voice 3:   We pray for the people of Asia
Voice 4:   We pray for the people of the Pacific

Voice 5:   We pray for the people of Europe

            *Some music is played or a chant sung as people come
            and light candles/night lights and place them centrally
            [in trays of sand!]*

Leader: Into the dark places of our world
           Where people are frightened and hungry
ALL: GOD BRING LIGHT, BRING LOVE

Leader: Into places where people are fighting
           Into places where people have no homes
ALL: GOD BRING LIGHT, BRING LOVE

Leader: Into the places where we feel unsafe
           Into situations that hurt us and scare us
ALL: GOD BRING LIGHT, BRING LOVE

Leader: We ask our prayers in Jesus' name
           and in the Holy Spirit's power
ALL: AMEN

           Song
           No-one will ever be the same

Closing responses

*Read alternately by each half of the congregation, e.g.
children/adults, left-hand side/right-hand side.*

A: God keep us safe in danger
B: Give us courage and keep us loving

A: God help us to speak the truth
B: To stand by those who need our help

A: God give us friends who love us
B: Places and people that help us grow

A: God send us on our way rejoicing
B: And welcome us safely home

ALL: AMEN

18   *An act of prayer*

For use when members of the Community gather and suitable for use in housegroups, meetings, etc.

Silence

The Community responses

Leader: The world belongs to God
ALL: THE EARTH AND ALL ITS PEOPLE
Leader: How good and how lovely it is
ALL: TO LIVE TOGETHER IN UNITY
Leader: Love and faithfulness meet
ALL: JUSTICE AND PEACE EMBRACE
Leader: If the Lord's disciples keep silent
ALL: THESE STONES WOULD SHOUT ALOUD
Leader: Open our lips, O God
ALL: AND OUR MOUTHS SHALL PROCLAIM YOUR
           PRAISE

Song and/or psalm

Prayer

Leader: Holy God, Maker of all
ALL: HAVE MERCY ON US
Leader: Jesus Christ, Servant of the poor
ALL: HAVE MERCY ON US
Leader: Holy Spirit, Breath of life
ALL: HAVE MERCY ON US
           Silence

Leader: I confess to God, and in the presence of all God's
           people, that I have sinned in thought, word and deed,
           and I pray God to have mercy on me.
ALL: MAY GOD HAVE MERCY ON YOU, PARDON AND
           DELIVER YOU FROM YOUR SINS AND GIVE YOU
           TIME TO AMEND YOUR LIFE.
Leader: Amen

ALL: WE CONFESS TO GOD, AND IN THE PRESENCE
          OF ALL GOD'S PEOPLE
          THAT WE HAVE SINNED IN THOUGHT, WORD
          AND DEED,
          AND WE PRAY GOD ALMIGHTY
          TO HAVE MERCY ON US

Leader: May God have mercy on you, pardon and deliver you
          from your sins, and give you time to amend your life.

ALL: AMEN

Leader: Turn again, O God, and give us life

ALL: THAT YOUR PEOPLE MAY REJOICE IN YOU

Leader: Make me a clean heart, O God

ALL: AND RENEW A RIGHT SPIRIT WITHIN ME

Leader: Give us again the joy of your help

ALL: WITH YOUR SPIRIT OF FREEDOM SUSTAIN US
          AMEN

Scripture reading

Followed by discussion, exposition or silence

Prayer for the Iona Community

Leader: O God, who gave to your servant Columba the gifts
          of courage, faith and cheerfulness, and sent people
          forth from Iona to carry the word of your gospel to
          every creature, grant, we pray, a like spirit to your
          church, even at this present time. Further in all things
          the purpose of our Community, that hidden things
          may be revealed to us, and new ways found to touch
          the hearts of all. May we preserve with each other
          sincere charity and peace, and, if it be your holy will,
          grant that a place of your abiding be continued still to
          be a sanctuary and a light, through Jesus Christ our Lord.
          AMEN

Prayer for our own reshaping

ALL: O CHRIST, THE MASTER CARPENTER,
WHO AT THE LAST, THROUGH
WOOD AND NAILS,
PURCHASED OUR WHOLE SALVATION,
WIELD WELL YOUR TOOLS IN THE WORKSHOP
OF YOUR WORLD,
SO THAT WE WHO COME ROUGH-HEWN TO
YOUR BENCH
MAY HERE BE FASHIONED
TO A TRUER BEAUTY OF YOUR HAND.
WE ASK IT FOR YOUR OWN
NAME'S SAKE. AMEN

Prayers for the members of the Iona Community

As listed for the day in Miles Christi

Leader: May they not fail you
ALL: NOR WE FAIL THEM
for the concerns of the Community,
• for the world

Prayers of thanksgiving

The Lord's Prayer

Leader: Lord, teach us to pray
ALL: OUR FATHER IN HEAVEN
HALLOWED BE YOUR NAME
YOUR KINGDOM COME, YOUR WILL BE DONE
ON EARTH AS IN HEAVEN
GIVE US TODAY OUR DAILY BREAD
FORGIVE US OUR SINS
AS WE FORGIVE THOSE WHO SIN AGAINST US
SAVE US FROM THE TIME OF TRIAL
AND DELIVER US FROM EVIL
FOR THE KINGDOM, THE POWER AND THE
GLORY ARE YOURS
NOW AND FOR EVER.
AMEN

Silence

Closing responses

Leader:	In work and worship
ALL:	GOD IS WITH US
Leader:	Gathered and scattered
ALL:	GOD IS WITH US
Leader:	Now and always
ALL:	GOD IS WITH US
	AMEN

RESOURCES

Beginnings and endings of worship

1

Come among us, Jesus

Come among us, Jesus
You whom the angels worship
and children welcome
COME JESUS, AND MEET US HERE

Come among us, Jesus
You who hurled the stars into space
and shaped the spider's weaving
COME JESUS, AND MEET US HERE

Come among us, Jesus
You who walked the long road to Bethlehem
and lit a flame that dances forever
COME JESUS, AND MEET US HERE

2 | *God, your constant love reaches the heavens*

God, your constant love reaches the heavens
Your faithfulness extends to the skies
YOUR RIGHTEOUSNESS IS TOWERING LIKE THE
MOUNTAINS
YOUR JUSTICE IS LIKE THE DEPTHS OF THE SEA
We find protection under the shadow of your wings
We feast on the abundant food you provide
YOU ARE THE SOURCE OF ALL LIFE
AND BECAUSE OF YOUR LIGHT, WE SEE THE
LIGHT
Psalms 36, vs 5-9 [1]

3 | *God of the past*

God of the past who has fathered and mothered us
WE ARE HERE TO THANK YOU

God of the future who is always ahead of us
WE ARE HERE TO TRUST YOU

God of the present here in the midst of us
WE ARE HERE TO PRAISE YOU

God of life beyond us within us
WE REJOICE IN YOUR GLORIOUS LOVE

4 | *Come God*

Come God
Come walk with your people
for you alone are our strength and glory
AND WE PUT OUR TRUST IN YOU

Come God
Come walk behind us, beside us, before us
for you alone are our shelter and direction
AND WE PUT OUR TRUST IN YOU

Come God
Come seek and find and put us right
for you alone are the light in our darkness
AND WE PUT OUR TRUST IN YOU

Come God
We know you are near
the sound of your footsteps sets us dancing
HELP US TO PRAISE AND WORSHIP YOU

5

For Christmas

Opening Responses

God of creation, shaper of seas and stars
of planets and of people
GOD IS HERE WITH US

God, born in Bethlehem
gurgling, crying, laid in a manger
GOD IS HERE WITH US

God, breath of the universe
flickering, dancing in the candle flame
GOD IS HERE WITH US

God, Immanuel, amongst us, within us
WE BRING OURSELVES AND OUR DREAMS
FOR WE WANT TO BE HERE WITH YOU

Closing Responses

Mysterious God, confounding our expectations
meeting us where we least expect to find you
STAY WITH US NOW

Child of the manger, healing our pain
sharing our weakness
STAY WITH US NOW

Source of life
birth of God within our own experience
STAY WITH US NOW

Stay with us in our frailty
stay with us on our journey
WALK BESIDE US, LIVE WITHIN US
LEAD US TO GLORY, LEAD US HOME

6 | *Opening responses for a liturgy for healing*

If you come
in certainty or in confusion
in anger or in anguish
THIS TIME IS FOR US

If you come
in silent suffering or hidden sorrow
in pain or promise
THIS TIME IS FOR US

If you come
for your own or another's need
for a private wound or the wound of the world
THIS TIME IS FOR US

If you come,
and do not know why,
to be here is enough
THIS TIME IS FOR US ALL

Come now, Christ of the forgiving warmth
Come now, Christ of the yearning tears
Come now, Christ of the transforming touch
THIS TIME IS FOR YOU

| 7 |

Name unnamed

Name Unnamed, whose intriguing presence
is closer to home than we dare imagine
fill us with wonder of you
THAT WE MAY BE FILLED WITH WONDER OF
OURSELVES

Name Unnamed, whose creativity is a river running
startle us with diversity
and surprise us with difference
THAT WE MAY BE FILLED WITH WONDER OF
OTHERS

Name Unnamed, whose mystery and concern is
revealed in Jesus
reshape our perceptions
reshape our patterns of living
reshape our politics and prayer
THAT WE MAY BE FILLED WITH WONDER OF A
WORLD MADE WHOLE

| 8 |

Invocation

From the corners of the world
from the confusion of life
from the loneliness of our hearts
GATHER US, O GOD

To feed our minds
to fire our imagination
to free our hearts
GATHER US, O GOD

9

Opening preparation for silent service

When the world tells us
we are what we do with
our activity, acumen or achievement
let us learn
WE ARE WHAT WE DO WITH OUR SILENCE

When the world tells us
we are what we do with
our spending power, selling power, or our power of
speech
let us learn
WE ARE WHAT WE DO WITH OUR SILENCE

When the world tells us
to drown the silent sufferings of others with indifference or noise
or to forget the art of stillness even in the storm
let us learn
WE ARE WHAT WE DO WITH OUR SILENCE

Where the world tells us
to rush in where angels fear to tread
let us learn that angels listen first
before they take a step
for the voice of God in the silence ...
Silence

1   Scriptures quoted from the *Good News Bible* published by
the Bible Society/HarperCollins Publishers, UK © American Bible Society, 1966, 1971, 1976, 1992, with permission

Short prayers

10 | *Stories*

Lord Jesus, you told great stories
they helped people make sense of their lives
they revealed God in ordinary things
they encouraged and changed people.

Make us more ready to share our stories
give us words where we are tongue-tied
confidence to know our stories matter
tact to know the right place to tell them.
Also, most importantly, make us ready to listen.

11   *Light*

Shining God
even the darkness is not dark to you
shine in our darkness, light of our lives

When we walk in the grey gloom of confusion
when pain drains all the colour out of life
when we are paralysed by the darkness of fear
shine in our darkness

When we know that others are walking in the darkness
give us courage to be light for them

12   *After Psalm 131*

God, you love us with a tender love
like Mary, holding her child gently in her arms
like Joseph, breaking with harsh tradition
to stand by his beloved and her baby.
Still our restless hearts to rest in you
knowing ourselves loved.

13   *Waiting*

God, so much of faith is waiting
like a pregnant woman waiting in hope
like a people under siege, holding out till relief comes
like the soul lost in the darkness,
unable to see even a glimmer of light
yet stumbling through the night because somewhere,
out ahead, day will surely break
God, be with us in our waiting

| 14 | · | *God of light and warmth* |

O God, star kindler
kindle a flame of love within us
to light our path in days of darkness

O God, sun warmer
warm us with your love
to melt the frozen hand of guilt

O God, moon burnisher
burnish the shield of faith
that we may seek justice
and follow the ways of peace

15   *Advent antiphons*

Traditionally, the Advent antiphons have been part of the
church's liturgy during the last week of Advent. They recall
people's experience of what God is like, and they call on God to
come to our aid. These prayers take their pattern and inspiration
from the antiphons of Advent.

> O God, you speak through your prophets
> your words hold us and challenge us and keep us right:
> come and tell us the truths that we need to know
> and write them into our hearts and lives.
>
> O Lover of the little ones,
> their Guardian and Defender:
> come with your angels and cradle your children
> and guide their stumbling feet
> along the homeward roads.
>
> O Maker of laughter,
> who plays with Leviathan in the deep waters:
> come stretch out your hands
> to cuddle and tickle your children
> through the moments of their days.
>
> O Loving Mother, whose presence offends many
> and delights many more:
> come and help us to see clearly
> the one in whose likeness we are made.
>
> O Pilgrim God, abandoning that which is no longer
> needed:
> come with us on our journey,
> show us how to travel lightly
> keeping only what we need to grow.

O God, you love us
come, come quickly,
We need your help.

O Wind of God, you blow through
the holes in our defences
and lay bare our fear:
come, breathe on us gently,
as at the beginning,
and give us life. [1]

16   ## *Creator God*

Creator God,
because you make all that draws forth our praise
and the forms in which to express it,
we praise you,
Because you make artists of us all,
awakening courage to look again at what is taken for
granted,
grace to share these insights with others,
vision to reveal the future already in being,
we praise you.
Because you form your Word among us,
and in your great work embrace all human experience,
even death itself, inspiring our resurrection song,
we praise you
yours is the glory

17   ## *Invocation for Lent*

Into a dark world
a snowdrop comes
a blessing
of hope and peace
carrying within it
a green heart
symbol of God's renewing love

Come to inhabit our darkness
Lord Christ,
for dark and light
are alike to you

May nature's white candles of hope
remind us of your birth
and lighten our journey
through Lent and beyond

18   *Invocation for Mothering Sunday*

Come, Mother God,
come as an enfolding
nurturing presence,
come as steadfast love
to hold us

Come, Mother God,
come as an enabling
strengthening force,
come as tough love
to let us go

Come, Mother God,
come as friend and comforter
healing our wounds
walking our way,
come as wounded healer
to make us whole

1   *A Book Of A Thousand Prayers*, edited by A Ashwin,
HarperCollins Publishers

Prayers for forgiveness

19

God of the spirit of kindness

God of the spirit of kindness,
in the glory of earth and sea and stars,
in the kaleidoscope of colour and shade and shapeliness,
in the patterns of humour and tenderness and touch,
we celebrate your generosity.

Forgive us when we forget the gift in our every breath,
the care that sustains our every moment,
that grace that can transform our every day.

Set us free from the prison of grudging hearts,
mean desires,
resentful spirits,
give us the courage to act with justice and generosity,
and draw us into love that does not calculate
or keep scores.

20 *Beloved God*

Beloved God
we fear your judgement:
teach us to know it as our friend.
Your word has pierced us to the bone;
we are exposed, laid open to your sight.

Therefore, let us bless you
for you come to us when we are most ashamed,
and when we long to hide our face from you
you will not suffer us to turn away.
You call us by our name
you touch us, raise us,
invite us into shameless love.
God our lover, know us, judge us,
turn us, wound us, demand of us,
forgive us.
We are yours.
We abandon ourselves to your love.
We trust you.

21 *Cross-carrying Jesus*

Cross-carrying Jesus
As you stagger on your lonely journey
time slips
worlds reel.
Forgive us that we turn away
embarrassed
uncaring
despairing.
Help us to stay with you through the
dark night
to watch and to wait
to know the depths of your anguish
and to realise that you carry us

forgive (even) us,
love us.
Forgive us
that we get on with our work unthinking
that we gamble unknowing with precious things.
Cross-carrying Jesus,
nailed to the tree of life,
forgive us
and grant us your salvation.

22 *This day*

Voice 1:   Cross-carrying Jesus
woodcarved to foul purpose
tree of life
deep rooted in Golgotha's soil
arms stretched to embrace the world
cross
empty
Christ let loose in the world.

Voice 2:   This day you will be with me in Paradise

Voice 3:   Who, me Lord?
Not me.
Not there.
I'm a thief.
I've stolen ladies' handbags
Young girls' virginity
I've diddled the books
and sold arms to Africa

Voice 2:   This day you will be with me in Paradise
Beyond death in new life you will walk with me
down our street
round the corner, with the chip papers
blowing in the wind and into the

betting shop.
You will dine at the Ritz
lie in the gutters of Calcutta
and step into outer space with confidence.

Voice 3:   Where, Lord?
Up there
or down here?
You confuse me.

Voice 2:   Come with me through the gates
and we shall see.

| 23 |

Lord of the morning

Bless to us, O God, this day, fresh made.
In the chorus of birds, bless us.
In the scent of blossom, bless us.
In the wet grass and the spring flowers, bless us.
Bless us and heal us
for we come to you in love and in trust.
We come to you in expectant hope.
Silence
O God, give us a well of tears
to wash away the hurts of our lives.
O God, give us a well of tears
to cleanse the wounds,
to bathe the battered face
of our world.
O God, give us a well of tears
or we are left, like arid earth,
unsanctified.
Silence

Heal us and your grieving world
of all that harms us.
By the power of your Resurrection
restore us to new life
set us on new paths
bring us from darkness to light
help us to choose hope.

Jesus says, 'Pick up your bed and walk'
pick up the bed of your sorrows and fears
pick up the bed of your grief and your sin
pick up your life and come, come follow Him.

| 24 |

On the side of justice

O God, you are on the side of justice
and you call your people to be on that side too.
Where people are turned off food-growing land
so a few can make big profits
where children work in factories for coppers
where women ruin their health to feed their families
not in the world of the past but the world of today
LORD HAVE MERCY UPON US,
CHRIST HAVE MERCY UPON US
God, forgive us if we profit from the suffering of
others
remind us that we have power in our choices
if we act together.
Lead us to choose justice,
in our politics, in our economics, in our churches.
Justice, beginning where we are ...

25 | *Rag and bone confession*

There are lumps under our carpet
that the hoover won't help
There are cats tied in bags
would be off like a flash
Skeletons in the cupboards
tap tap on the doors
There is nothing hidden
but that's going to get out
So let's get it over with, God
Silence
There's a pile at the foot of the cross
of the things we could do without
Make us glad we brought them to you
who carries away the sins of the world
and grant in their place
pardon and grace
and your call to be following always.

26 | *Confession*

Together in worship, we face what we might not face
alone
— that we are greedy, but fail to love our bodies
— that we are selfish, but fail to love ourselves
— that we are lazy, but fail to work for peace
— that we are human, but fail to love the earth
these we share in silence as we remember
our own faults and failings ...
Silence
God of the turning tide
change us so that the energy of your forgiveness
flows into bold and joyful action
into a humility which is not defeatism
into the strength and confidence to be vulnerable.

27 *Your Kingdom come*

Lord,
you know that we love you
and we know what you ask us to do ...
but for those times when we have been too busy
when we have been hard-hearted
when we have been lukewarm
we say sorry
and ask, for your forgiving love
Prepare us for your way, O Lord
YOUR KINGDOM COME, YOUR WILL BE DONE

Lord,
you know our good intentions
and we know your will ...
but hold us back long enough to listen to those in need
                        and to learn from them
                        and to learn of our own need
Where we think we are sent, make us ready to receive,
where we are keen to teach, make us ready to learn.
Prepare us for your way, O Lord
YOUR KINGDOM COME, YOUR WILL BE DONE

Lord,
you know our deepest desires
and we know the vision of your Kingdom ...
we bring before you those elements in our lives
in need of your transforming power:
that which we misuse or neglect,
that which we most reluctantly let go of,
that which we believe is not good enough:
inspire us and disturb us to examine our deepest desires.
Prepare us for your way, O Lord
YOUR KINGDOM COME, YOUR WILL BE DONE

Lord
you know our potential
but what is your purpose for our lives?
In our uncertainty
and in the knowledge of your faithfulness,
prepare us for your way, O Lord
YOUR KINGDOM COME, YOUR WILL BE DONE

28 *Creator God*

Creator God
by your design we are whole people
yet we have sought to prise Word from flesh
to drain truth from life
we have lived in our limits
touching the bounds for reassurance
we have distrusted the vision
and sought to destroy the visionary
KYRIE ELEISON/LORD HAVE MERCY
said or sung

Forgive us
when we have been willing to be entertained
but not changed
when we have allowed our insights
to harden into cliches
when we have spoken
only to consolidate our own position
when we have called on you
only to hear the sound of our own voices
when our celebrations have left others
with nothing to enjoy
KYRIE ELEISON/LORD HAVE MERCY

Searching and creative Spirit of God
who makes community
from the raw materials of our lives
teach us the humility to learn from those
who know a true rejoicing
through Jesus Christ
who simply revealed your glory [1]

1   From *The Book of Common Worship* © 1993 Westminster/
     John Knox Press. Used by permission of Westminster/John
     Knox Press.

Words of faith

29 *Adoration*

We cannot tell
how much the sound of silence,
creation's beauty, gloriously aflame;
we cannot tell
how much the sight of starlit heavens
moves us to prayer,
to praise creation's Maker,
and our own.

We cannot tell
how much the son of Mary
the man of Nazareth,
the son of God upon a tree;
we cannot tell
how much the man of sorrows
moves us to prayer,
to praise the One
who gives our lives
a meaning and a goal.

We cannot tell
how much the Spirit's comfort,
how much the wind of freedom
means to us.
We cannot tell —
for words cannot contain
the love beyond all loves,
the truth
that in the end
there is
only
God.

30 ## *After Psalm 19*

The sky does it simply, naturally
day by day by day
the sun does it joyfully
like someone in love
like a runner on the starting-line
the sky, the sun,
they just can't help themselves
no loud voices, no grand speeches
but everyone sees, and is happy with them.

Make us like that, Lord
so that our faith is not in our words but in our lives
not in what we say but in who we are
passing on your love like an infectious laugh:
not worried, not threatening, just shining
like the sun, like a starry night,
like a lamp on a stand,
light for life —
your light for our lives.

31 *Birth*

To wait
to endure
to be vulnerable
to accept
to be of good courage
to go on
day after day after day;
to be heavy with hope
to carry the weight of the future
to anticipate with joy
to withdraw with fear
until the pain overcomes
the waters break
and the light of the world
is crowned.
Then the travail is over
joy has overcome.

Lord of heaven and earth,
crowned with blood
at your birth,
delivered with pain,
bring new hope to birth
in your waiting world
bring fresh joy
to those who weep.
Be present
in all our dyings and birthings.

| 32 | ## *Lifted high*

A little kid ran across the street
runny-nosed, a bit scruffy
tripping over almost.
She ran towards a man whose
arms were opened wide to
welcome her.
'Give us a swing Jesus,' she said,
and she felt herself lifted high
and she saw the street and the sky whirling
around her, ablaze with colour,
like a mixed-up rainbow.
She was laughing then —
excited, free
gasping for breath
'enough' she said
and she felt herself slowing down
relaxing, safe, as Jesus
held her in his arms
and smiled ...

Unless we become like little children
Unless we risk that joy and abandonment
Unless we run and ask and let ourselves
be lifted high

We are never going to enter the Kingdom of God

33   *Lent darkness*

Dragons lurk in desert spaces
penetrating the mind with evil claw.
Serpent's teeth seek out the chinks
insidiously, relentlessly, gnawing on the bone;
searching out the interstices of muscle and sinew.

Such is the pain of the wilderness.
Alone, alone, alone,
Christ sits
in the waste place of abandoned pleas and questions
until exhausted
finally
at last
the realisation
comes
that in the end
there is only
God.

In the night-time of our fears
in the present reality of abandonment
when family and friends
turn and run,
be present, ever present God.
Be present with those
camped out in the fields of hopelessness
with refugees and homeless,
those who live lives of quiet desperation.
Be present until the desert places
blossom like the rose
and hope is born again.

34 *Coming home*

Written for someone joining the church
When you cross the borders of the desert
and head for home
you do not want to turn back.
What you are heading for is a place of belonging
a place where you can lay your body down
Everything inside you is running
you have run away often
but this time you are running for home

You will still be yourself
still be restless sometimes and afraid
but what beckons you now are bonds of loving
and, when all is said and done,
(and sometimes there is too much saying and too little
doing)
living where your life belongs is coming home
Welcome to the family

35 *For my Mother*

'Underneath are the everlasting arms'
loved words and loving —
reminding us of a God
who is always there,
like a mother with a young child,
knowing our needs,
catching us when we fall,
comforting, bearing, cradling, dancing and caressing.

Underneath are the everlasting arms:
words of encouragement
in moments of desolation
and loneliness;
words passed down from mother to daughter,
not in cold print but warm with faith.

Underneath are the everlasting arms:
now you are dying —
is it hard to let go?
For so long you have been there
to catch, to carry and to care.
Listen, love, I want you to know
that I can cope:
first your faith nurtured me,
and your strength,
but now I have found my own.
Let go.
Into God's hands I commend your spirit:
Underneath are the everlasting arms.

36   *Circuit*

Based on a prayer from the Carmina Gadelica
I make my circuit
in the fellowship of my God
on the machair, in the meadow,
on the cold heathery hill,
on the corner in the open,
on the chill windy dock,

to the noise of drills blasting,
to the sound of children asking.

I make my circuit
in the fellowship of my God
in city street
or on spring-turfed hill,
in shop-floor room
or at office desk.

God has no favourite places.
There are no special things.
All are God's and all is sacred.
I tread each day
in light or dark
in the fellowship of my God.

Be the sacred Three of glory
interwoven with our lives
until the Man who walks it with us
leads us home
through death to life.

Thanksgiving

37 *Thanksgiving for community*

Thank you for our time in community
for deep, if fleeting, friendships
for those conversations late at night
for the vulnerable intensity lubricated by laughter
for the freedom to serve others
and to affirm ourselves
in the face of all that you know and we know of our
lives
and we thank you for any signs that the churches
with which so many are disaffected
can yet be your body on earth in the community of
creation

38 | *Thanksgiving prayer*

Thanks be to you, God awesomely distant
thanks for the searing of shooting stars
the colours of the planets in the night sky
the space and power beyond our perceiving
which sparkles the sky of our lives with your caring.

Thanks be to you, God uncomfortably close
giving life to dead dry things
— the dance of pure stillness,
the beat of our hearts,
is your doing.

Thanks be to you, God known in a body
who blessed as he lived
who raised up our life
to be gathered as one, reaching out for the kingdom.

39 | *Hope growing*

Hope growing,
silently, secretly,
like a child in the womb, fluttering;
putting out soft fingers,
hope, stretching, stirring.

Hope growing,
silently, secretly,
daring to breathe again
as footsteps recede
and danger retreats,
hope, stretching, stirring.

Hope growing,
silently, secretly
swelling, burgeoning, bursting
until the flower opens
the child is crowned,
the prisoner is released
and hope is born.

God of all hopefulness,
for seeds of silent growth
and secret expectation,
we thank you.
Bring hope to birth in us;
release us that we may worship
in freedom and joy.

40 *All shall be well*

For the greening of trees
and the gentling of friends
we thank you, God.

For the brightness of field
and the warmth of the sun
we thank you, O God.

For work to be done
and laughter to share
we thank you, O God.

We thank you, and know
that through struggle and pain
in the slippery path of new birth
hope will be born
and all shall be well.

| 41 | ### *Thanksgiving*

Gracious God
for your love for us
gentle as a shower
healing our pain
binding our wounds
WE GIVE YOU THANKS

For your love for us
sure as the dawn
transforming our darkness
revealing your truth
WE GIVE YOU THANKS

For your love for us
mercifully steadfast
calling us to you
raising us up
WE GIVE YOU THANKS

For your love for us
encouraging questions
open to doubts
making us vulnerable
WE GIVE YOU THANKS

Urge us on, O Christ
to find wholeness
through serving you
by serving others
in the power of your Spirit

42 *Midwife of our lives*

God of power and presence
you are the midwife of our lives,
always drawing us on to be born again,
encouraging, exhorting, calming,
containing even death.
You pull us, kicking, into life,
breath spirit into us.
We thank you for the gift in our breath,
the love that we make,
the hope that we cherish,
the grace that encompasses our darkest day.
In smallness and splendour, in storm and serenity,
we celebrate your care and creativity.
We rest in you, as trustingly as any baby.

43 *Jesus our faithful friend*

Jesus our faithful friend
we thank you for the precious gift of friendship
for the people who accept us as we are
love us even in our least attractive moments
help us laugh at ourselves and laugh at life
encourage us, support us, believe in us, value us.
Help us never to take friendship for granted
but to tend it as a beautiful plant.

44 *Lord Jesus, it's good to know*

Lord Jesus, it's good to know
that you lived in the flesh
walked where we walk, felt what we feel,
got tired, had sore and dirty feet,
needed to eat, and to think about
where the next meal was coming from.

But it's even better to know
that you enjoyed your food
the feel of perfume on your skin
the wind on your face, a child in your arms
and the good wine at the wedding.

You didn't mind when people touched you,
even those who were thought of as unclean.
You kissed people with diseases
and laid your head on your friend's shoulder.
Thank you for understanding our bodily pains and
pleasures
and for valuing them.

| 45 | ### Great thanksgiving

*When this prayer is used, the words of institution are
said in the invitation to the Lord's table, or in relation
to the breaking of the bread.*

Holy God, we praise you.
Let the heavens be joyful
and the earth be glad.

We bless you for creating the whole world,
for your promises to your people Israel,
and for Jesus Christ, in whom your fullness dwells.

Born of Mary, he shares our life.
Eating with sinners, he welcomes us.
Guiding his children, he leads us.
Visiting the sick, he heals us.
Dying on the cross, he saves us.
Risen from the dead, he gives new life.
Living with you, he prays for us.

With thanksgiving we take this bread and this cup
and proclaim the death and resurrection of our Lord.
Receive our sacrifice of praise.
Pour out your Holy Spirit upon us
that this meal may be
a communion in the body and blood of our Lord.
Make us one with Christ
and with all who share this feast.
Unite us in faith,
encourage us with hope,
inspire us to love,
that we may serve as your faithful disciples
until we feast at your table in glory.

We praise you, eternal God,
through Christ your Word made flesh,
in the holy and life-giving Spirit,
now and forever. Amen.

Concern

46

Praying for more

God, Creator,
more than mother, more than father,
in love you spoke,
and there was the world
for which we now pray.

We pray for more than our speech can contain:
for trees and mountains,
fish and birds,
the species that come and go over time.

We pray for more people than we can ever meet,
and because we pray,
you can ask us to share your peace
with the victims of war.

And because we pray,
you can ask us why farmers are paid
not to grow crops
while sisters and brothers go hungry.
And because we pray,
you can ask us why our creative gifts are used

to destroy families and nations
and the world around us.

You can ask us,
because you know from experience
what our life is like,
so our prayer is a two-way talk.

And we pray,
in our world,
get your word in edgeways

47   *New ways*

God of our lives
you are always calling us
to follow you into the future,
inviting us to new ventures, new challenges,
new ways to care,
new ways to touch the hearts of all.
When we are fearful of the unknown, give us courage
When we worry that we are not up to the task,
remind us that you would not call us
if you did not believe in us.

When we get tired,
or feel disappointed with the way things are going,
remind us that you can bring change and hope
out of the most difficult situations.

| 48 | *Moving house*

'When the removal men left,
table and chairs were still
out in the yard.
We had so many belongings —
far more than we needed.'

Holy Spirit,
for whom there is room in every home,
help to clear a way

through the clutter of possessions,
to make room for those who live there
to be fully themselves,
and for outsiders to be welcomed.

Spirit of hospitality, bless all
who share meals at our table —
even if it's still
out in the yard.

49   *Neighbours*

God with us,
you did not put us in the world alone
you gave us people to live beside
to keep us company
to share skills and resources
to stop us from getting bored.
Thank you for good neighbours
people who are kind, people who are funny,
people who notice if something is wrong
people we trust enough to leave our keys with.
God beside us,
sometimes we don't like our neighbours
we can't believe you really meant them
when you said, 'love your neighbours,'
did you God?
Not the nosey or noisy ones,
not the messy ones,
not the ones whose children don't behave
whose dress or manners we don't like?

If you really do mean them, God
we're going to need your help.
Help us not to be too quick to judge.
Help us to hold out a hand of friendship
help us to remember that loving our neighbours
is not what we feel, but what we do.

The shadow of the dove

When dawn's ribbon of glory around the world
returns
and the earth emerges from sleep —

May the shadow of the dove be seen
as she flies across moor and city.
Over the warm breast of the earth she skims,
her shadow falling on the watcher in the tower,
the refugee in the ditch,
the weary soldier at the gate.

May the shadow of peace
fall across the all-night sitting of a council
across the tense negotiators around a table.

May the shadow of hope
be cast across the bars of a hostage cell
filling with momentary light
rooms tense with conflict,
bringing a brief respite,
a slither of gold across the dark.

May she fly untiring across flooded fields,
across a city divided by hate and fear,
across a town wreathed in smoke.

May the shadow of reconciliation,
the dove of peace with healing in her wings,
be felt and seen and turned towards
as she makes righteousness shine like the dawn,
the justice of her cause like the noonday sun.

Holy Spirit of love
BRING HEALING, BRING PEACE

51   *Thomas*

Put your hand,
Thomas,
on the crawling head
of a child
imprisoned
in a cot
in Romania.
Place your finger,
Thomas,
on the list of those
who have disappeared
in Chile.

Stroke the cheek,
Thomas,
of the little girl
sold in prostitution
in Thailand.
Touch, Thomas,
the gaping wounds
of my world.
Feel, Thomas,
the primal wound
of my people.
Reach out your hands,
Thomas,
and place them at the side of the poor.
Grasp my hands, Thomas,
and believe.

Prayer rosary

Hiroshima,
Bosnia,
Belfast,
the names slip through our fingers
like bloodstained beads.

As we tell the story,
tell us,
tell us,
tell us,
the way
to peace.

Beirut,
Nagasaki,
Nuremberg,
still they come, countless numbers:
people hounded, refugees tramping the road
out of hell, into hell.

Where will it stop?
Show us,
show us,
show us,
the way to peace.

Five for sorrow,
ten for joy.
May what has been sown in pain
be reaped in hope.

53 | *Prayer for Hiroshima Day: August 6th*

God, today in sorrow, we remember and we share our grief.

The few seconds of annihilating time
at Hiroshima and Nagasaki that seared itself forever
into the depth of our present existence.
Those who died, those who wish they had died
and those who live never to forget:
WE REMEMBER

The many thousands all over the world
who sighed with relief at the ending
of six long years of war.
Those who died,
those whose suffering made them long for death,
those whose experiences seared their lives
and hopes forever,
those who waited, mourned,
and lived lives of regret at home:
WE REMEMBER

The scientists, politicians, engineers, technicians
and members of the armed forces
who came to realise the awesome power and
responsibility of new technology,
and who live with the results of that knowledge:
WE REMEMBER

The present generation,
growing up in a changed world
overshadowed by the threat of extinction,
feeling helpless in the web of events:
WE REMEMBER

We acknowledge our share of the pain and the responsibility.

God, in Christ you showed us
that you are not removed from us
but share in our agony and suffering.
You are the mother holding her child from the blast,
you are the tortured prisoner longing for release,
you are the war-weary soldier,
you are the scientist pacing the midnight hour,
you are the child with nuclear nightmares,
you know and suffer our human condition.

We know that nothing can separate us from your love.
We pray for your love to enfold us in comfort
your love to share our agony
your love to inspire us to love one another
your love to live in hope.

| 54 | *Prayer for lesbian and gay people*

Gracious God
We pay for gays and lesbians
who often face the fears and prejudices of a hostile
world
and church

We pray for lesbians and gays
who often face discrimination in the workplace,
marketplace,
and in the place of worship

We pray for gays and lesbians
who often face the risk of being outed, hunted,
shunned, shamed, shouted and preached at

We pray for lesbians and gays
who often face for good or ill dubious findings
in science, politics, social research and theology
We pray for lesbians and gays
who often dare to bring a range of gifts
and the courage to be themselves into the community
of the Way

55 · *At a wedding*

God is love
and those who live in love
live in God.

Love-giving God
who created us in your image
who walked with us in a garden
heard our laughter, our quarrels
promised us heirs and a community of hope
God who brought us forth
nurtured and fed us
taught us to walk and run and grow
made us for each other,
let your love surround and lead
Name and *Name* today and always.

Love-making Christ
Carpenter, Teacher, Friend,
who changed water into wine at weddings
cracked jokes about camels
and took upon yourself the heavy yoke
of the world's sins:
Christ alive — in our lives
in our community
in our world
let your love embrace and reconcile
Name and *Name* today and always.

Loving Spirit
whose breath soft as butterfly wings
can move mountains
whose fire can cleanse and renew
Spirit vibrant with joy and peace
let your love comfort and challenge
Name and *Name* today and always.

56 *Lord of weddings*

Lord of weddings where the ordinary took on
an extra special flavour
May *Name* and *Name* taste the rich wine of your love.
Let their love be a
listening
forgiving
honest
caring
sharing
a sharing of delight and chores
of good times and bad
may they go out now with confidence
into the community as a new creation.
Lovers — made in your image.

57	### *For mourners*

Let us pray for those who mourn

God, loving *Name*
nearer to us than our next breath
be with those who mourn.
Be in their shock, their grief,
their anger and despair
that they may grieve,
but not as those without hope.

Forgive all the harm they/we feel
they/we have done to *Name*
and show them that they/we are forgiven.

We offer to you
all the regrets
the memories
the pain
the 'if onlys'
knowing that you
will surround those we mourn
with your presence
and heal them and us
of all that harms us.

| 58 | *Prayers for a funeral*

In the silence of our hearts
we bring before God *Name*
to thank God for her/his whole life
and to remember her/him.

We remember *Name* as a child and young adult
Add details of parents, siblings, place, etc.
Silence
We remember *Name* making his/her way in the world
especially *(add details of work, family, public life)*
Silence
We remember *Name*'s enjoyment of *(add interests,*
pursuits)
and his/her skills at *(add skills, accomplishments)*
Silence
And we remember and give thanks for all *Name* was
—his/her *(strength/warmth/courage/care for others*
or other attributes of personality)
Silence
As we remember and give thanks for *Name*'s life,
so we also remember ourselves
and we bring to God our sorrow, our sense of loss, our
grief
Silence
And we bring to God the harder feelings we may have
over this death
Help us to forgive any hurt *Name* has caused us
and forgive us
for any hurt we may have caused *Name*.
Silence
God who holds us all with arms of love and compassion
knows all we feel and endure at this time
and accepts and invites us to lean upon these arms,
through Jesus Christ our Lord

59   *After a bereavement*

God of all life
when all there is in our lives
is the empty space where the beloved was
and nothing can fill it
and we want nothing to fill it
because nothing, and no-one, can take the place
of the beloved,
and we walk drearily through the days,
dragging one foot after the other
and there is no joy in anything,
give us your strength in our sorrow,
your presence in the absence we feel,
your rest, that we may rise again to new life,
and your hope, that in death we are not divided.

God of all life,
when your people are mourning,
make us patient listeners
to the memories of happy times
make us sensitive carers
so that we support but do not weaken
make us good friends,
so that we can hold the future open
for when our friends are ready to face it,
and hear our prayers for those recently bereaved ...

| 60 |

Surrounded by a cloud of witnesses

Each occasion
we glimpse them:
that turn of a head,
that smile,
the way she walked,
his sense of humour,
each time
a knife turns
in our heart.
In time,
through the windows of our tears
we see them
and smile.
In time,
we let go of sorrow.
In time,
beauty and music,
remembered places
bring solace not pain.
In your time,
God of all time,
may what we have sown in pain
be reaped in joy.

61   *Communion of saints*

God of grace
we thank you for the saints whom we ourselves
have known and loved.
It does not come easily to us to call them saints,
it seems as if ordinary mortals
are not good or great enough,
but you have given your people this name
and invited us into your company
and you know how much we loved them.
So for these good companions,
whom we name before you for their love,
and for our love of them,
we give you grateful thanks *(Names ...)*

In the mystery of your love
in the power of your spirit
we are one with them
We give great thanks.

62   *'As you love yourself'*

We pray for those who do not love themselves
who cannot face the turmoil in their souls
who put themselves down and call it selflessness
who make themselves ill with bitterness
who become sick with self-loathing.
Restore them and help them to live with themselves
that they may joyfully live with each other.
And we pray for ourselves,
for the times when 'they' include us.

63

Prayer for prophets

Almighty God,
in whose prophets through the ages
we have seen your truth clearly outlined,
we pray for people of vision in our day
those who carry undimmed
the light of the longing for justice
those who speak in the councils of nations
to persuade and convince
those who lead and support in action groups,
political parties and networks
those who resist blind power and risk persecution
to show a new way.

We pray for people in the front line of change,
newspaper editors, politicians, poets
and people who are called to explore a common future,
for prophets of speech and pen, canvas and lens,
for artists who are not afraid to look
and tell what they see,
who name what is deadly
and call us to new birth,
who trust their imagination
so that we may live life to the full.

Litanies and responses

64 *As winter trees*

As winter trees
stretch out bare arms to a dark sky
WE STRETCH OUT IN THE DARKNESS
TO FIND THE TOUCH OF LOVE

As snowdrops
turn their gentle faces to the sun
WE LONG TO FIND IN THAT WARMTH
THE PROMISE OF PEACE

As the fire
breaks the shell of the seed
SO MAY OUR PAIN BREAK THE SHELL OF ISOLATION
THAT PROTECTS US FROM OURSELVES

In the security of darkness
the warmth of sunshine
the promise of fire
MAY WE BLOSSOM ANEW
IN THE MIRACLE OF YOUR SAVING LOVE
O GOD

65

Wellspring of our lives

Creator Spirit, wellspring of our lives,
as the refreshing rain falls on the just and unjust alike
REFRESH US WITH YOUR MERCY, WHO KNOW
OUR OWN INJUSTICE

As a stream flows steadily on, defying all the odds of
stone and water
FLOW OVER EVERY BOUNDARY AND BORDER
THAT SEPARATES US FROM EACH OTHER

As the waters of our baptism washed us and welcomed us
RENEW US NOW IN NEWNESS OF LIFE AND UNITY
OF LOVE

As we were once held in the waters of our mothers'
womb
HOLD US IN THE POWER AND PEACE OF YOUR
ABIDING PRESENCE

66

Responses for a burial

Into the darkness and warmth of the earth
WE LAY YOU DOWN

Into the sadness and smiles of our memories
WE LAY YOU DOWN

Into the cycle of living and dying and rising again
WE LAY YOU DOWN

May you rest in peace, in fulfilment, in loving
MAY YOU RUN STRAIGHT HOME INTO GOD'S
EMBRACE [1]

| 67 |

Responses for a cremation

Into the freedom of wind and sunshine
WE LET YOU GO

Into the dance of the stars and the planets
WE LET YOU GO

Into the wind's breath and the hands of the starmaker
WE LET YOU GO

We love you, we miss you, we want you to be happy
GO SAFELY, GO DANCING, GO RUNNING HOME [2]

| 68 |

God's wisdom

Lord Jesus, Teacher,
this is what you want us to learn,
not the world's wisdom, but God's,
and so we pray
awaken us to our need of you in our lives
AND YOU WILL GIVE US YOUR LIFE

Move us with sorrow for the sorrow of the world
AND YOU WILL MAKE US STRONG THROUGH
OUR TEARS

Give us the humility to admit our failures
AND YOU WILL BRING TREASURE OUT OF THEM

Make us hungry for justice
AND YOU WILL GIVE US FOOD THAT LASTS

Help us to see others through your eyes
AND YOU WILL SHOW US OURSELVES WITH LOVE

Show us how to practice what we preach
AND WE WILL SEE GOD IN EVERYONE

Support us in standing firm for truth, even when it costs
AND THE TRUTH WILL ALSO MAKE US FREE

1-2   *A Book Of A Thousand Prayers*, edited by A Ashwin,
       HarperCollins Publishers

Cursings and blessings

69 *How terrible*

A: How terrible for us
     when we ignore the presence of strangers
B: How terrible for us
     when the sick and the old remain lonely
A: How terrible for us
     when the little ones are hurt or ignored
B: How terrible for us
     when the prisoner is deemed beyond redemption or love
A: How terrible for us
     when we do not question laws
     that reward the strong and put down the weak.
B: How terrible for us
     when we know what we should do,
     and we walk the other way
A and B: How terrible for us,
           for we bring God's anger upon ourselves
           and we walk into outer darkness.

(Based on Matthew 25)

70

Cursed be

Cursed be garbage in an open sewer
Cursed be the barbed wire of camps
Cursed be the gassing and maiming of children

71

May the Maker's blessing be yours

May the Maker's blessing be yours
encircling you round
above you
within you

May the angels' blessing be yours
and the joy of the saints
to inspire you
to cherish you

May the Son's blessing be yours
the wine and the water
the bread and the stories
to feed you
to remind you

May the Spirit's blessing be yours
the wind, the fire
the still small voice
to comfort you
to disturb you

And may my own blessing be yours
a blessing rooted in our common pilgrimage
the blessing of a friend

72 | *Blessing and laughter and loving*

Blessing and laughter and loving be yours
the love of a great God
who names you
and holds you
while the earth turns and the flowers grow
this day
this night
this moment
and forever. [1]

73 | *Bless to us, O God*

Bless to us, O God
the doors we open
the thresholds we cross
the roads that lie before us.
Go with us as we go
and welcome us home.

74 | *The love of the faithful Creator*

The love of the faithful Creator
The peace of the wounded Healer
The joy of the challenging Spirit
The hope of the Three in One
surround and encourage you
today, tonight and forever.

75 | *As you have been fed*

As you have been fed at this table
go to feed the hungry.
As you have been set free
go to set free the imprisoned.
As you have received — give.
As you have heard — proclaim.
And the blessing which you have received
from Father, Son and Holy Spirit
be always with you.

76 | *As you were*

As you were in the ebb and flow,
as the beginning becomes the ending,
and the ending a new beginning,
be with us
everpresent God.

77 | *Wherever we go*

Wherever we go,
may the joy of God the gracious
be with us.
Wherever we go,
may the face of Christ the kindly
be with us.
Wherever we go,
may the compassing of the Spirit of grace
be with us.
Wherever we go,
the presence of the Trinity around us
to bless and to keep us.

78   *We have laid our burdens down*

We have laid our burdens down
in the presence of the living God.
We have been nourished for our journey
in the presence of the living God.
We have taken on the armour of Christ
in the presence of the living God.
Now lead us, guide us, defend us,
as we go into your world
in your name and for your sake,
O loving, living God.

1   *A Book of A Thousand Prayers*, edited by A Ashwin,
     HarperCollins Publishers

Reflections, readings and meditations

Walking on the water

Biblical Reading: Matthew 14, vs 22-33.
This monologue may be used as a reflection on the
Biblical reading in worship on the theme of faith, trust
and risk-taking.

He'd told us to cross the lake —
to go on home in the boat
and to leave him with the crowd on the shore.

I'd not wanted to do that.
We were, after all, his protectors;
without us there, who was to stop the people staying
with him all night,
wearing him out, demanding of him
more stories and cures and miracles?
But he'd insisted,
and given us no choice.
I'd no idea how he was intending to get home —
it was a long walk, and a lonely one.

It turned into a bad night.
A storm blew up —
it came out of nowhere,
and we were sailing straight into it.

The waves slapped against the sides of the boat,
the cold spray showering over us,
soaking us to the skin.
It was a night of nightmares.

And then the screams —
someone shouted out that they could see a man
walking towards us through the water —
a ghost,
a trick of the moonlight,
the spirit of a long drowned sailor,
our imaginations ran riot.

And then a voice came out of the darkness,
a human voice,
a voice we knew
shouting through the storm —
'have courage, it's me, don't be afraid.'

There was a silence then, a strange silence,
as if the waves were waiting to see how we would
answer.

I heard myself speaking.
'Master, if it is you,
if it's really you,
tell me to come to you across the water.'

Another silence,
and then a single word —
a word that filled me with terror and delight —
'Come.'
I climbed over the boat's side
and I walked towards him.
I felt like a child again
balancing dangerously along the top of a high wall,
full of laughter and of pride.
I had nearly reached him,
when I felt the wind pulling at me,
buffeting me,
and I looked around me, into the darkness,
and I panicked, and I sank
splashing and spluttering into the cold waves.

At once, he had hold of me,
telling me to trust him,
carrying me back to the boat.

I remember laying there,
curled up on the deck,
catching my breath,
clutching at the wet mast,
still feeling the strength of his body close to mine.

The wind had dropped by then,
and the others were sitting at his feet,
hardly able to look up at him.
One of them, trying to make sense of it all,
told him that he must be God's son.
He did not reply.

As we sailed eastwards,
towards the dawning light,
the waves rocked us gently,
reassuringly,
as if God's hand were cradling us,
strengthening us,
soothing away our fears.

80 *If you want to*

*A man suffering from a dreaded skin disease came to
Jesus, knelt down and begged him for help. 'If you
want to' he said, 'you can make me clean.' Jesus was
filled with pity and stretched out his hand and touched
him. 'I do want to' he answered. 'Be clean.' At once the
disease left the man, and he was clean.*
(Mark 1, vs 40-43) [1]

'If you want to.'
Of course Jesus wanted to,
for his prayers and his actions were rooted in love,
the love of God
that set him free to be vulnerable and to care and to
live.

Of course he wanted to.
Love always wants the best for other people,
be they lepers
mothers-in-law, strangers or friends,
love always wants their lives to be whole and glad and free.

And of course he wants us to.
For in our streets and communities
it is our hearts and lives he uses
to make his love and his healing and his justice real.
It is through how we live and what we do
that good news and good things come to other people.

And today he wants us to.
For he is here among us
and it is our hands and our prayers
through which he comes to us and to those we pray for.
And it is his love,
born and alive in us,
that will heal us and set us free.

81 | *The outsiders*

Appropriate Biblical references may be used.

Voice 1:   I am not respectable —
a single parent
bringing the burden
and blessing of my children
into the presence of the disciples,
those grey-suited men
who are, of course,
uniformly respectable.

Voice 2:   I am not respectable —
I handle money,
I get my hands dirty,
I don't always get it right.
Am I accountable?
Whom do I really serve?
People feel cheated by the system.
I am part of the system.
I am only human ...
and I handle money.

Voice 3:   I am not respectable —
a woman of a certain age
with womb problems.
Period.
I'm not good company

(hysteria, you say)
intense, sometimes distressed,
disconcerting, undermining
your sense of what is decent and godly:
unclean.

Voice 4: I am not respectable —
I have an illness
you would rather not mention,
never mind touch
with your tidy lives.
How did I get into this mess?
Whose fault was it?
Why do I persist
in calling attention to myself
and believing in healing?

Voice 5: I am not respectable —
I was caught in the act.
They have all abandoned me:
my husband,
my lover ...
I am alone
and ashamed.
I am at the mercy
of the righteous people
whose clean hands are full of stones.

Voice 1-5: We are not respectable —
we are poor, unemployed,
ill, in the wrong,
old, outsiders.
How did we come to be among you?
How can we expect your awareness,
never mind your acceptance?

Voice 1:   We are not respectable —
            and yet we are welcomed
            by Jesus
            who turns to listen to our voices,
            who reaches out
            to touch us
            with hands he is not afraid to get dirty,
            to embrace us;
            who, in the moment of accepting us
            for who we are
            shows us that we are forgiven
            and worthy of respect.

1   Scriptures quoted from the *Good News Bible* published by the Bible Societies/HarperCollins Publishers UK © American Bible Society, 1966, 1971, 1976, 1992, with permission

82 *Nunc Dimittis*

May be used as a lead-in meditation for the Nunc
Dimittis.
Biblical reading: Luke 2, vs 22-38

It happened that
an old man and an old woman saw a word one day
a word that looked familiar
a word they thought they had seen many times before
an insignificant word and one of many like it
that had passed in front of their eyes that day

not a word to write home about
not even a particularly well-presented word
and probably not a word you'd find in better circles
·just a rather scruffy word wrapped up in a small cloth parcel

but as they looked
a curious thing happened
they knew that this was the word
that they had been waiting for all these years
they knew that this was the word
that might fill the world with new talk
they knew that this was the word
that would make sense of all words
they didn't know how they knew ... they just knew!

After they had managed
to catch their breath from surprise
the old woman rushed out to tell anyone
who cared to listen about the word she had seen
she sang a song about how this word
would change everything
the old man held the word
in his tired but trembling hands
and he also sang a song from the top of his heart

The word was brought to the temple
by Mary and Joseph
The old woman was Anna —
the prophetess in the temple
The old man was Simeon
whose song we now say/sing together

Lord now let your servant go in peace ...

| 83 | *Yorkhill and Yarrows*

Our fourth child Colin was born with a harelip and cleft palate. When he was about nine months old, he went into Yorkhill Children's Hospital in Glasgow for an operation on his lip.

He had his operation on a Monday morning; on Tuesday, the wee soul looked as though he'd had a fight with Frank Bruno. I still remember his accusing eyes, how, even puffed-up and half - closed, they managed to convey his bewilderment and offence. It was almost as though he were asking, 'Why are you letting this happen to me? Why am I suffering? Why don't you do something, my daddy?'

And it's so hard to take, for no matter how much you love the child, you are impotent to answer or take away the pain.

As I left the hospital that morning, I found myself thinking about the offence of life; thinking of the vast numbers of my sister and brother human beings for whom life is an offensive puzzle. The suffering children of Africa sprang immediately to mind, as do the many suffering children around the world today.

To the humiliated, the abused and the oppressed of the world, surely life is an offence ... and that cannot be God's will; cannot be the will of the God whose demand for justice is like a drumbeat running right through the Bible.

As I left the hospital that Tuesday morning, despite my discomfort at being unable to do anything for Colin, I was full of admiration for the surgeon's skill, the nurses' care and the dedicated and cheerful work of the myriad of ancillary workers. My mind boggled, and still boggles, at the array of magical and wonderful tools of the healing people, the X-ray machines, the dialysis machines, the lasers, the microscopes, even the humble drips which are so often, literally, life-givers. The fruits of our modern technology.

I left Yorkhill Hospital that Tuesday morning to go to Yarrows, the famous warship builders on the River Clyde, where I was the industrial chaplain. Here was another community of people, men and women whose incredible skills, imagination and inventiveness was every bit as wonderful as those of the hospital. From being among the hospital workers, nurses and doctors who make up a community of healing, I was now among a community of workers whose great skills were being used to create the tools of death ... for sadly, that's what warships are, and once we've built them, the best we can hope for is that they will never be used.

The contrast between what we ask decent, hardworking folk to do at Yorkhill and Yarrows struck me so clearly that day ... and has never left me.

'The war to end all wars' has been fought, and still from here to the furthest-flung corners of the globe, the clamour for more and more and better and better arms continues unabated.

The dream of creating 'a land fit for heroes' has been dreamt, and still old men sleep under railway arches, children are abused, women despair.

When will we ever learn?

The great prophets of old consistently told of the fate of those who put their trust in chariots. They were doomed.

We do well to listen to the ancient word.

'Do you not know? Have you not heard
The Lord is the everlasting God:
he created all the world.
He never grows tired or weary.
No one understands his thoughts.
He strengthens those who are weak and tired.
Even those who are young grow weak;
young men fall exhausted.
But those who trust in the Lord for help
will find their strength renewed.
They shall rise on wings like eagles;
they will run and not get weary;
they will walk and not grow weak.'

This is the word of the Lord. We do well to listen.

I attended the launch of a Type 22 Frigate, the last of its kind, HMS Cumberland.

She was launched by the Princess of Wales. Intoning the traditional words, 'I name this ship Cumberland. May God bless her and all who sail in her,' she cracked the bottle of champagne on the magnificent bow. The shipwrights down below knocked away the crucial stocks, and, so slowly at first, but quickly gathering momentum, she slid into the water, the environment for which she was created.

When the time came for her finally to leave the yard, she sailed down the river, a magnificent and awesome sight, armed to the teeth with all the latest and most sophisticated weapons that modern technology can produce. There was no denying her beauty, nor the pride in the building of her, yet the best that we could hope for was that she should never fire her mighty guns in anger; that one day she would go to the scrapyard with every missile on board still in its silo.

84 | *Women at the riverside*

Exodus 2, vs 1-11

A: I am a Levite woman,
wife of a Levite man.
I carried his child
safe in the secret cradle of my womb
for nine months, afloat
in the waters of life,
until the day the waters broke
and he swam out into a dangerous world.
For three more months, I hid him in our hut,
but his little voice grew stronger
so one day I took a basket
woven of rushes that grow at the water's edge,
I daubed on tar to make it watertight,
a little coracle, then took it down,
to float where the river lapped among the reeds.

B: I am his sister,
a small solemn child
standing by the side of a big river
to see what will happen.
I see the river, wide, lazy, slow-moving, life-bearing,
with the sun glinting on its smooth surface.
I cannot see our little cradle-boat
but I know it is there, hidden among the whispering reeds
with my baby brother.
I am a big sister, with a huge responsibility.
I see strangers coming down to the beach
to play, as though they haven't a care in the world,
to bathe in the river.
I see a great lady, one of our enemies.
Can she see the baby? What will she do?
My legs turn to water;
my eyes fill with tears.

C: I am Pharaoh's daughter.
I left the stale air of the palace,
the baking courtyards and colonnades,
the passions of politics,
the hard facts of life, the reasons of state.
I walked with my women
on the bare earth,
down to where the river offers
another way of being,
with its cool flow, its gentle caress, its feelings.
I wanted freedom to be myself
in another element,
and I fell for a baby.

D: I am a slave girl.
All I did was wade in deep
and fetch an ordinary basket
from where it was hidden in the rough reeds.
Did I guess its secret?
What did I feel,
as I held it, trembling,
and heard the hungry cries?
Who hears my voice?

C: I was moved with pity
by the tears of the baby.
I knew it must be a Hebrew child,
and suddenly, there at my elbow,
was another child:
not asking for money
like your normal urchin, but offering help
'do you want a nurse for the baby?'
The child has sense — a wise child.
I suspect there's more in this than meets the eye:
a story I don't know, an alien experience,
a strange and powerful torrent of feeling.
I accepted her help.

B: I called my mother, like a stranger.
A: I came and nursed my child, who knew me.
D: I found him, as lost as myself.
C: I adopted him, and called him Moses
        because I drew him out of the water.

A: We are the women: a wife
B: A sister
C: A daughter
D: A slave —
        women without names
All: But we are the ones
        who trusted the child
        to the strange and saving waters
        and drew him out alive
        and called him by name.

Author index for liturgies:

Author index for resources:

Index of songs

All published by Wild Goose Publications, Glasgow

BE NOT AFRAID
BY THE WATERS OF BABYLON
FOR THE HEALING OF NATIONS
THOSE WHO WAIT ON THE LORD
UBI CARITAS (TAIZE)
WE LAY OUR BROKEN WORLD
The above songs are not published by Wild Goose Publications, but are widely anthologised.

O GOD, THOU ART THE FATHER
ALMIGHTY FATHER OF ALL THINGS THAT BE
from *The Church Hymnary*, 3rd Edition, OUP 1973

THE LOVE BURNING DEEP
from *Love Burning Deep*, by Kathy Galloway, SPCK 1993

GOD GIVE US POWER
HALLELUJAH, WE SING YOUR PRAISES
IPHARADISI
from *Freedom Is Coming*, edited by Anders Nyberg, Utryck, Uppsala and available in the UK from Wild Goose Publications

The Iona Community

The Iona Community was founded in 1938 by the late Lord MacLeod of Fuinary (the Rev. George MacLeod DD). It was initially a movement for renewal in the Church of Scotland. The rebuilding of the ruined cloistral buildings of Iona Abbey (completed, through a combination of professional and voluntary work over nearly thirty years, in 1967) provided a powerful focus for the specific concerns of the Community: the integration of work and worship, politics and prayer, and the development of new forms of worship, of the common life, of youth work, of the ministry of healing, and of experiments in mission.

The Community today is a movement of some 200 members, 1,200 associates and 2,000 friends. It describes itself as 'an ecumenical community, within the Church of Scotland, of men and women seeking new ways of living the Gospel in today's world.' Its members are committed to a rule of daily prayer and Bible study, sharing and accounting for the use of their money and their time, meeting together, and action for peace and justice in the world.

The Community maintains three centres of work, worship, and the common life on Iona and Mull, and administrative offices in Glasgow.

For information on the Iona Community please contact:

The Iona Community,
Pearce Institute,
840 Govan Road, Glasgow G51 3UU

T. 0141 445 4561; F 0141 445 4295.
The following are available:
- Membership details
- A Deed of Covenant form
- Information about volunteering on Iona
- A catalogue of publications

Other titles available from WGP

SONGBOOKS with full music (titles marked * have companion cassettes)
THE COURAGE TO SAY NO; 23 SONGS FOR EASTER & LENT*John
 Bell and Graham Maule
GOD NEVER SLEEPS – PACK OF 12 OCTAVOS* John Bell
COME ALL YOU PEOPLE, Shorter Songs for Worship* John Bell
PSALMS OF PATIENCE, PROTEST AND PRAISE* John Bell
HEAVEN SHALL NOT WAIT (Wild Goose Songs Vol.1)* J Bell & Graham
Maule
ENEMY OF APATHY (Wild Goose Songs Vol.2) J Bell & Graham Maule
LOVE FROM BELOW (Wild Goose Songs Vol.3)* John Bell & G Maule
INNKEEPERS & LIGHT SLEEPERS* (for Christmas) John Bell
MANY & GREAT (Songs of the World Church Vol.1)* John Bell (ed./arr.)
SENT BY THE LORD (Songs of the World Church Vol.2)* John Bell (ed./arr.)
FREEDOM IS COMING* Anders Nyberg (ed.)
PRAISING A MYSTERY, Brian Wren
BRING MANY NAMES, Brian Wren

CASSETTES & CDs (titles marked † have companion songbooks)
Tape, THE COURAGE TO SAY NO † Wild Goose Worship Group
Tape, GOD NEVER SLEEPS † John Bell (guest conductor)
Tape, COME ALL YOU PEOPLE † Wild Goose Worship Group
CD, PSALMS OF PATIENCE, PROTEST AND PRAISE † Wild Goose
 Worship Group
Tape, PSALMS OF PATIENCE, PROTEST AND PRAISE † WGWG
Tape, HEAVEN SHALL NOT WAIT † Wild Goose Worship Group
Tape, LOVE FROM BELOW † Wild Goose Worship Group
Tape, INNKEEPERS & LIGHT SLEEPERS † (for Christmas) WGWG
Tape, MANY & GREAT † Wild Goose Worship Group
Tape, SENT BY THE LORD † Wild Goose Worship Group
Tape, FREEDOM IS COMING † Fjedur
Tape, TOUCHING PLACE, A, Wild Goose Worship Group
Tape, CLOTH FOR THE CRADLE, Wild Goose Worship Group

DRAMA BOOKS
EH JESUS...YES PETER No. 1, John Bell and Graham Maule
EH JESUS...YES PETER No. 2, John Bell and Graham Maule
EH JESUS...YES PETER No. 3, John Bell and Graham Maule

PRAYER/WORSHIP BOOKS
PRAYERS AND IDEAS FOR HEALING SERVICES, Ian Cowie
HE WAS IN THE WORLD, Meditations for Public Worship, John Bell
EACH DAY AND EACH NIGHT, Prayers from Iona in the Celtic Tradition,
Philip Newell
IONA COMMUNITY WORSHIP BOOK,
WEE WORSHIP BOOK, A, Wild Goose Worship Group
WHOLE EARTH SHALL CRY GLORY, THE, George MacLeod

OTHER BOOKS
EXILE IN ISRAEL: A Personal Journey with the Palestinians, Runa Mackay
FALLEN TO MEDIOCRITY: CALLED TO EXCELLENCE, Erik Cramb
REINVENTING THEOLOGY AS THE PEOPLE'S WORK, Ian Fraser
WHAT IS THE IONA COMMUNITY?